GNS3 Network Simulation Guide

Acquire a comprehensive knowledge of the GNS3 graphical network simulator, using it to prototype your network without the need for physical routers

"RedNectar" Chris Welsh

BIRMINGHAM - MUMBAI

GNS3 Network Simulation Guide

First published: October 2013

Production Reference: 1211013

Published by Packt Publishing Ltd.
Livery Place
35 Livery Street
Birmingham B3 2PB, UK.

ISBN 978-1-78216-080-9

www.packtpub.com

Cover Image by Chris Welsh (rednectar.chris@gmail.com)

Credits

Author
"RedNectar" Chris Welsh

Reviewers
Anthony Burke

John Herbert

Acquisition Editor
Wilson D'souza

Commissioning Editor
Sruthi Kutty

Technical Editors
Monica John

Nikhil Potdukhe

Faisal Siddiqui

Project Coordinators
Romal Karani

Esha Thakker

Proofreader
Lucy Rowland

Indexer
Tejal R. Soni

Production Coordinators
Melwyn D'sa

Alwin Roy

Cover Work
Melwyn D'sa

About the Author

"RedNectar" Chris Welsh likes to share knowledge, so it's no surprise that he spends most of his time teaching, some of his time consulting and too much of his time on forums and blogs. The teaching is mainly Cisco related (he became a CCSI in 1998), the consulting is through his own company (Nectar Network Knowledge) and his blog (`http://rednectar.net`), along with his contributions to the GNS3 Forum (`http://forum.gns3.net`), became the inspiration to write this book. To keep his sanity, he likes to go for long walks in bushland, particularly around the National Parks near his hometown of Sydney, Australia.

About the Reviewers

Anthony Burke is an Enterprise Network Architect in the Australian emergency services sector. He has experience across many technology and business verticals. Anthony is very passionate and driven in seeking out technology trends and abstracting the business application. He has more than 5 years of experience in the industry, is currently Cisco and Juniper certified, and is undertaking the path to CCIE and eventually CCDE.

Anthony contributes back to the community by blogging at `blog.ciscoinferno.net` and various other platforms. Anthony can be found on twitter as `@pandom_`

> I would like to thank my loving wife Katrina. You rock! I thank you for indulging me and listening to me when I start rambling about the benefits of OSPF versus EIGRP or why the industry hasn't shifted to IPv6 yet!

John Herbert, CCIE® #6727 (Routing and Switching) has been moving packets around networks for over 15 years, and has been doing so as a consultant since 1999. In his spare time, he blogs at `http://lamejournal.com/` and can be found on Twitter as `@mrtugs`. John lives in Atlanta, Georgia with his wife and three children, and has a home network that is arguably the very definition of *overkill*.

www.PacktPub.com

Support files, eBooks, discount offers and more

You might want to visit www.PacktPub.com for support files and downloads related to your book.

Did you know that Packt offers eBook versions of every book published, with PDF and ePub files available? You can upgrade to the eBook version at www.PacktPub.com and as a print book customer, you are entitled to a discount on the eBook copy. Get in touch with us at service@packtpub.com for more details.

At www.PacktPub.com, you can also read a collection of free technical articles, sign up for a range of free newsletters and receive exclusive discounts and offers on Packt books and eBooks.

http://PacktLib.PacktPub.com

Do you need instant solutions to your IT questions? PacktLib is Packt's online digital book library. Here, you can access, read and search across Packt's entire library of books.

Why Subscribe?

- Fully searchable across every book published by Packt
- Copy and paste, print and bookmark content
- On demand and accessible via web browser

Free Access for Packt account holders

If you have an account with Packt at www.PacktPub.com, you can use this to access PacktLib today and view nine entirely free books. Simply use your login credentials for immediate access.

Table of Contents

Preface 1

Chapter 1: Clearing the First Hurdle 7

Pre-installation tasks and prerequisites 8

Understanding the GNS3 family of applications 8

Memory and CPU 9

Router image files 9

Downloading GNS3 11

The installation process 11

Installing on Windows 11

Installing on OS X (Macintosh) 12

Installing on Linux Mint 13

Post-installation tasks 14

The setup wizard 15

Summary 19

Chapter 2: Creating your First GNS3 Simulation 21

Jumping in the deep end – a basic two-router configuration 22

Conceptualizing a project 28

The topology.net file 28

The configs directory 29

The working directory 29

Opening a project 29

Getting to know the GUI 30

Tips for managing your workspace 31

Tips for managing your routers 32

Using VPCS (Virtual PC Simulator) 32

Capturing packets with Wireshark 37

Avoiding the 100 percent CPU utilization problem 39

Coming to grips with Idle-PC values 40

Introducing GNS3 generic switches   **42**
   Ethernet switch   42
   Frame-relay and ATM switches   45
Summary   **46**

Chapter 3: Enhancing GNS3   **47**
Connecting to physical interfaces   **48**
   Mini-project – connecting your GNS3 router to your LAN   48
     Why can't my host computer ping my router?   51
   The Microsoft Loopback adapter   52
   The Linux NIO TAP adapter   52
   The OS X TUN/TAP adapter   55
Adding VLAN support   **59**
   Generic Ethernet switch   59
   EtherSwitch router   60
Terminal tips   **61**
   Using a different terminal application   62
   Using the AUX port   63
   Troubleshooting a device console   63
Fine-tuning the topology – adding graphics and text   **64**
Accessing GNS3 running on a remote machine   **64**
   Accessing a device console remotely   65
   Linking GNS3 topologies on different hosts   66
Summary   **66**

Chapter 4: Unleashing Other Emulators   **67**
The Qemu emulator   **68**
   Adding Qemu support   68
     Linux   68
     Qemu preferences   69
   Microcore Linux using Qemu   70
   Adding ASA firewalls   73
   Adding Juniper routers (Junos)   78
The VirtualBox emulator   **84**
   Adding VirtualBox support   84
   A Windows PC on Oracle VirtualBox   85
   A Linux PC on VirtualBox   89
   Adding a Vyatta router using VirtualBox   89
Summary   **95**

Chapter 5: The Cisco Connection   **97**
Cisco routers – emulated hardware   **97**
Cisco IOS   **99**
     Platform   100

Feature set   101
Memory location and compression format   101
Train number   101
Maintenance release   101
Train identifier   101
RAM requirements and the feature navigator   102
Summary   **103**

Chapter 6: Peeking under the GNS3 Hood   **105**
Understanding the topology.net file   **105**
Say hello to the hypervisor   **107**
The GNS3 orchestra   **110**
UDP tunnel concept   112
Conducting Qemu and VirtualBox   115
Debugging using the GNS3 management console   **117**
Summary   **118**

**Chapter 7: Tips for Teachers, Troubleshooters,
and Team Leaders**   **119**
Packaging your projects   **120**
Adding instructions   120
Managing snapshots   121
Using remote hypervisors   **121**
Remote hypervisor tutorial   121
Preparing the remote servers   122
Preparing the host computer   123
Load balancing across multiple hypervisors   126
Using your local GNS3 host as a hypervisor   126
Building the topology   126
Choosing the right platform   127
Using VPCS with remote hypervisors   127
Running GNS3 in a virtual machine   **128**
The GNS3 WorkBench solution   129
GNS3 Limitations   **131**
Ethernet interfaces are always up   131
Cisco router support   132
Host PC communication in a virtual machine environment   132
Getting more help   **132**
Official websites for all the GNS3 suite of programs   132
Other helpful online resources   133
Summary   **134**

Index   **135**

Preface

GNS3 is a Graphical Network Simulator that allows the user to run multiple emulated systems including Cisco routers, Juniper routers, Vyatta routers, Linux virtual machines, and Windows virtual machines. Getting GNS3 to actually do this simulation is not always an easy task, especially if you wish to venture beyond a simple network topology.

This book explains exactly what GNS3 does and how to harness that power to build anything from simple CCNA style router simulations to powerful integrated topologies using multiple operating systems across multiple computers.

Topics are covered in a tutorial fashion, so you can work with the author and build your own simulated topologies as you read.

What this book covers

Chapter 1, Clearing the First Hurdle, will take you through the simple installation and post installation tasks required to build your first GNS3 simulation.

Chapter 2, Creating your First GNS3 Simulation, takes you through some important background concepts that will help you get the most out of GNS3, even if you have used GNS3 before, and culminates with a Cisco router simulated network.

Chapter 3, Enhancing GNS3, will explore some of the more advanced features of GNS3, the place to come for help with a particular need, some of which will be prerequisites for later exercises.

Chapter 4, Unleashing Other Emulators, shows you how to use the other GNS3 emulators, Qemu and Oracle Virtual Box and between them how to emulate Cisco ASAs, Juniper Junos routers, Vyatta routers, Linux computers, and Windows computers.

Chapter 5, The Cisco Connection, deals with the routers that are supported by GNS3 and how to find the right iOS with the features you need.

Chapter 6, Peeking under the GNS3 Hood, deals with the internal communications between GNS3, Dynagen, Dynamips, Qemu, and Oracle Virtual Box.

Chapter 7, Tips for Teachers, Troubleshooters, and Team Leaders, shows you how to build a lab with multiple copies of GNS3/Dynamips working together in a variety of ways, along with some detailed troubleshooting tips.

The bonus online chapter, *Preparing for Certification using GNS3*, will provide tips and exercises that will be useful for you, no matter what level of certification you are going for. This chapter is available at `http://www.packtpub.com/sites/default/files/downloads/0809OS_Chapter 8_Preparing_for_Certification_using_GNS3.pdf`.

What you need for this book

To complete the examples in this book you will need a computer running Linux, OS X, or Windows, and copies of any operating system required to emulate Cisco routers, Juniper routers, Vyatta routers, Linux virtual machines, or Windows virtual machines.

 It is the responsibility of the user to ensure that the devices he/she chooses to emulate have valid software licenses.

You will also need an internet connection to download your copy of GNS3 and any other associated software and scripts as described in the book.

This book was written using computers running Linux Mint Version 15.0 (Cinnamon), OS X Version 10.8.4 (Mountain Lion), and Windows 8.0. The GNS3 version used for development was 0.8.4, with some enhancements not officially seen till Version 0.8.5. Other versions and installation variations may produce slightly different results to those displayed in this book.

Who this book is for

This book is written to assist networking professionals who need to prototype networks, and candidates preparing for their networking exams (for example, CISCO certified exams among others) in getting the best use out of GNS3. This book assumes a good level of competency using computers and basic configuration of the devices that they will simulate.

Conventions

In this book, you will find a number of styles of text that distinguish between different kinds of information. Here are some examples of these styles, and an explanation of their meaning.

Code words in text, IP addresses, folder names, filenames, file extensions, pathnames, and dummy URLs are shown as follows: "After downloading the `checkpic.sh` script from `http://forum.gns3.net/download/file.php?id=2019`, store it in your `~/GNS3/Images` directory."

A block of code is set as follows:

```
#!/bin/bash
sudo tunctl -t tap0
sudo ifconfig tap0 0.0.0.0 promisc up
sudo brctl addbr br0
```

Any command line input or responses that you need to enter are italicized within text or code blocks, such as:

To configure the Cisco ASA syntax, start with the *enable* command and use the following as a guide:

ciscoasa> *enable*

Password: *<Enter>*

ciscoasa# *configure terminal*

ciscoasa(config)# *interface gigabitEthernet 0*

ciscoasa(config-if)# *nameif outside*

New terms and **important words** are shown in bold. Words that you see on the screen, in menus or dialog boxes for example, appear in the text like this: "Navigate to **File | New Blank Project** to reach the **New Project** dialogue."

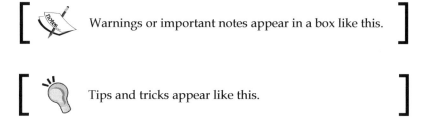

Warnings or important notes appear in a box like this.

Tips and tricks appear like this.

Reader feedback

Feedback from our readers is always welcome. Let us know what you think about this book—what you liked or may have disliked. Reader feedback is important for us to develop titles that you really get the most out of.

To send us general feedback, simply send an e-mail to feedback@packtpub.com, and mention the book title via the subject of your message.

If there is a topic that you have expertise in and you are interested in either writing or contributing to a book, see our author guide on www.packtpub.com/authors.

Customer support

Now that you are the proud owner of a Packt book, we have a number of things to help you to get the most from your purchase.

Errata

Although we have taken every care to ensure the accuracy of our content, mistakes do happen. If you find a mistake in one of our books—maybe a mistake in the text or the code—we would be grateful if you would report this to us. By doing so, you can save other readers from frustration and help us improve subsequent versions of this book. If you find any errata, please report them by visiting http://www.packtpub.com/support, selecting your book, clicking on the **errata submission form** link, and entering the details of your errata. Once your errata are verified, your submission will be accepted and the errata will be uploaded on our website, or added to any list of existing errata, under the Errata section of that title. Any existing errata can be viewed by selecting your title from http://www.packtpub.com/support.

Piracy

Piracy of copyright material on the Internet is an ongoing problem across all media. At Packt, we take the protection of our copyright and licenses very seriously. If you come across any illegal copies of our works, in any form, on the Internet, please provide us with the location address or website name immediately so that we can pursue a remedy.

Please contact us at copyright@packtpub.com with a link to the suspected pirated material.

We appreciate your help in protecting our authors, and our ability to bring you valuable content.

Questions

You can contact us at questions@packtpub.com if you are having a problem with any aspect of the book, and we will do our best to address it.

1
Clearing the First Hurdle

This chapter gets you through the first hurdles you will strike in your quest to have a **Graphical Network Simulator** (**GNS3**) running on your computer, and it comes in three parts: pre-installation tasks and prerequisites, the installation process, and the post installation tasks required to build your first simulation. During the process, you will gain an appreciation of the other applications and pieces of software that all contribute to make GNS3 work. I will explain the reasoning behind the multiple steps you need to take to install GNS3 successfully and finish the chapter with you well-prepared to build your first simulation emulating Cisco routers.

The following topics will be covered in this chapter:

- Pre-installation tasks and prerequisites:
    - Router image files
    - Downloading GNS3

- The installation process:
    - Installing on Windows
    - Installing on OS X
    - Installing on Linux Mint

- Post installation tasks

By the end of this chapter you should have GNS3 running on your computer ready to create your first network simulation.

Pre-installation tasks and prerequisites

The first prerequisite is that the installer realizes that GNS3 is not a normal application! It is a collection of inter-working applications and hosted operating systems, each with their own memory and CPU demands. You are not going to get GNS3 installed and running as quickly as you might some other standalone application.

But you probably already know that – I'm guessing that you are reading this book because you have at least already installed, or attempted to install GNS3, and struck a point at which you realize you need to know more. To address this, I will start with some essential knowledge that will help you see the bigger picture. If you are new to GNS3 or new to network simulation concepts, you would do well to read the `http://gns3.net/` home page before you continue.

Understanding the GNS3 family of applications

GNS3 can be thought of as a meeting place for a variety of operating system emulators. The best known and most important of these is **Dynamips**. Dynamips allows you to emulate Cisco routers and provides a collection of generic devices and interfaces.

Other emulators supported by GNS3 are the following:

- **Qemu**: This provides emulation of Cisco ASA devices, Juniper Routers, Vyatta routers, and Linux hosts.
- **Pemu**: This is a variation of Qemu used expressly for Cisco PIX firewalls.
- **VirtualBox**: This provides emulation of Juniper Routers, Vyatta routers, Linux hosts, and Windows hosts.

Every instance of a router or any other device you run is going to spawn a copy of its own operating system that will compete for your host computer's RAM and CPU cycles. You will be running multiple computers within your computer, so remember that as your computer's CPU heats up and your fans begin to whirr more loudly.

Now consider that devices like routers and firewalls require some kind of terminal application to give you access, so meet the next member of the GNS3 extended family, your terminal application. Depending on your operating system, your terminal application might be Gnome Terminal, iTerm2, Konsole, PuTTY, SecureCRT, SuperPutty, TeraTerm, Windows Telnet client, or even Xterm.

No matter which terminal application you choose, it will consume some more resources for every session you have opened, although it is minimal.

Finally, there are two more companion applications that are not essential, but often used in conjunction with GNS3. These applications are as follows:

- **Wireshark**: This is a popular open source packet-capture application.
- **Virtual PC Simulator (VPCS)**: This allows you to simulate up to nine PCs that you can use to ping, traceroute, and more.

And of course, these too need CPU and RAM when you use them.

So before you start thinking about running GNS3 on your computer, you had better make sure that it is up to the job, but that will largely depend on how many devices you plan to include in your simulations, how much memory you allocate to these devices, and how well you are able to "tune" the Idle-PC value (discussed in *Chapter 2, Creating your First GNS3 Simulation*).

I have successfully run GNS3 with a single router on a Pentium IV based computer with 1.5GB RAM. Running two routers on the same computer is possible, but slower.

Memory and CPU

I'll cut to the chase. You need as much memory as you can afford. I wouldn't want to run GNS3 on less than 2GB RAM and I'd buy 16GB or more if I could afford it. And router emulation can be CPU intensive. Quad core CPU would be awesome, but a Pentium IV could get you started. Multi-core CPUs are especially useful if you intend to use Qemu or VirtualBox emulators.

That said, if you want to be more precise, you should be able to calculate how much of your RAM is being consumed by your Operating System itself, with as few other programs as possible running, then add the amount of RAM that GNS and the associated programs consume, and finally add the amount of RAM you will allocate to your devices.

Router image files

The most important pre-installation task for GNS3 is to have a **router image** file ready. This is often the task that causes people to give up on GNS3 before they get started, but it is necessary because *Dynamips* (or *Qemu* or *VirtualBox*) is nothing more than an emulator, and it is going to need an operating system image to emulate!

For example, if you plan to emulate Cisco 3725 router, your image file might be called `c3725-adventerprisek9_ivs-mz.124-25b.bin`.

Note: Obtaining the appropriate image files for your router is your responsibility. It may be necessary to buy a piece of the hardware you wish to emulate and copy the image files from the hardware you own.

Whatever your image file(s) are, prepare for your installation by copying your image files to the appropriate locations as listed below. You will need to create the GNS3 and Images directories as you go.

Operating System	Location for the image files
Windows	%HOMEPATH%\GNS3\Images\
OS X or Linux	~/GNS3/Images/

If you have a maintenance contract with Cisco, you can download router images for your router from the Cisco Software Centre. If you have an ASA device, you will probably find copies of the software on the accompanying CD, or again you can obtain software for devices from Cisco, provided you bought a maintenance contract.

For Cisco routers I recommend using Cisco 7200 or 3725 router images. Most of the examples in this book will use the Cisco 3725 router because it requires no configuration to get started. For serious simulations, I would recommend using 7200 routers because the 7200 is the model for which Dynamips was designed, and this router also supports Cisco IOS (Internet Operating System) Version 15.

The story is similar for Junos – the operating system for Juniper routers. You can find the Junos software easily on the Juniper website, but you'll need to use your customer login to download the software.

Downloading Vyatta router images is much easier because Vyatta is an open source project. You can download both Qemu and Virtual Box based Vyatta router images directly from the GNS3 sourceforge.net download page: http://sourceforge.net/projects/gns-3/files/ - look in the Qemu Appliances or VirtualBox Appliances directories. However, getting a Vyatta router working is much more complicated than the Cisco routers discussed here. Deploying Vyatta routers is discussed in *Chapter 4, Unleashing Other Emulators*.

Now, if you have one or more router images in your Images directory as described previously, you are ready to install GNS3. The following examples will assume you have a Cisco 3725 router image in your Images directory.

Downloading GNS3

Depending on your operating system and which features you want to use, you may need to download more than a single application to get GNS3 running. However, there is no better place to start than at the GNS3 website: `http://www.gns3.net/download/`.

Not only will you find links to the latest GNS3 downloads for Windows, OS X (Macintosh) and Linux, but also a list of links to some of the other associated software you might need.

The installation process

The installation process is vastly different for each operating system. If you are running a version of Windows, the only installation package you need is the **all-in-one** package – although getting it installed and running may require a little more work. For OS X and Linux users, your tasks are going to be much more detailed.

Installing on Windows

Download and install the all-in-one package from `http://www.gns3.net/download/`. During the installation process you will get the chance to choose the packages you wish to install.

I recommend that you choose to install SuperPutty during the installation. It will then become your default console application, otherwise PuTTY will be your default console application. However, be warned that SuperPutty will download and install the .NET framework the first time it runs (it is huge and takes a long time) and requires a restart as well.

During the installation you will need to confirm any Windows UAC challenges or license agreements you may be confronted with, and in the case of Windows 8 you may even be presented with a compatibility issue when WinPcap is installed. If so, simply choose to **Run the program without getting help**.

Once the installation is complete, go ahead and begin the *Post-installation tasks* in this chapter.

Installing on OS X (Macintosh)

There is no **all-in-one** package for OS X, so you have to find the bits you need and install them one at a time. Here is what you will need to download in addition to GNS3. Use the latest version, and for the installation process, I will assume that the following applications have been downloaded.

Application	Download from...
XQuartz X11	`http://xquartz.macosforge.org/landing/`
Wireshark	`http://wireshark.org/download.html`

Step 1: Install XQuartz X11

With OS X, it is best to install Wireshark before GNS3, but Wireshark uses an X11 display, so first you have to install X11. XQuartz is the X11 version created by the XQuartz community project created by Apple.

Open the XQuartz install `.pkg` file, accepting all the agreements and entering your password when required.

When your XQuartz installation is completed, you will have to log out and log in again. I suggest running XQuartz after logging back in (it gets installed in the `/Applications/Utilities` directory) to be sure the install went smoothly. You should see an Xterm window open.

Step 2: Install Wireshark

I recommend you install Wireshark before GNS3. This is because, as explained in the `Read me first.rtf` document, Wireshark installs:

> `/Library/StartupItems/ChmodBPF`. *A script which adjusts permissions on the system's packet capture devices (/dev/bpf*) when the system starts up.*

Having these permissions is going to make life easier when you install GNS3.

Wireshark comes as a `.pkg` install file. But (on Mountain Lion at least,) your default security preferences will prevent you from installing it. To bypass the security preferences, you must launch the install package by right-clicking (or <*Ctrl*>-clicking) on the package and selecting **Open**. Accept all the agreements and enter your password when required.

Run Wireshark when the installation is finished. When you first run Wireshark, it will ask for the location of your X11 application – which is **XQuartz**.

Click on the **Browse** button and locate XQuartz in `/Applications/Utilities/`. You will then have to quit Wireshark and run it again, being patient as it builds its cache.

> Note: Wireshark always starts XQuartz when it runs, and you will need to switch to the XQuartz window rather than the Wireshark window when you switch between applications.

Step 3: Install GNS3

Open the GNS3 `.dmg` you downloaded, where you will find a single application – GNS3. Drag the GNS app to your Applications directory to install it.

However, your `GNS3.app` is more packed away than just GNS3. Not quite an all-in-one package like Windows, but it does include a copy of Dynamips and VPCS, which you will use soon, as well as a copy of the Qemu emulator which you will use later.

Once the installation is complete, go ahead and begin the *Post-installation tasks* section.

Installing on Linux Mint

There are many variations of Linux, but when it comes to software distribution, there are two main installation flavors – `rpm` (based on Red Hat) and `deb` (based on Debian). Since there is actually a way to install GNS3 from a `deb` package, I have chosen to use Linux Mint 15.0 (Cinnamon) desktop as the principle flavor of Linux to describe the installation process. This process should also work on other flavors of Debian Linux including Ubuntu. For other Linux flavors like Red Hat, check out the GNS3 Forum and go ahead, ask for help if you need it.

Step 1: Prepare your repository

The GNS3 source files are now stored in a **Private Package Archive (PPA)**. Before you can use the PPA, you must first give your Linux system permission to use it. From a Linux command line, issue the following command to prepare your system to use the GNS3 PPA. At the same time, you should ensure that your repository is up-to-date by running **apt-get update** from a terminal command window.

sudo add-apt-repository ppa:gns3/ppa

sudo apt-get update

Step 2: Install Dynamips and GNS3

Before you install GNS3 you must be sure that Dynamips is installed first. The following command ensures you get the latest of both and will also install Wireshark.

sudo apt-get install gns3 dynamips

Step 3: Install VPCS

As with the other packages, VPCS is also part of the PPA and is installed in the same way as shown:

sudo apt-get install vpcs

Step 4: Install Xterm

GNS3 requires Xterm to run VPCS and the **Tools | Terminal** command. Xterm is often installed by default on Linux, so the following command will update your install to the current version if it is already installed, or install it if it is not.

sudo apt-get install xterm

You are now ready to proceed to the post-installation tasks.

Post-installation tasks

No matter which OS you installed GNS3 on; the next task is to run GNS3. The **Setup Wizard** will appear.

Note: When GNS3 starts, it looks for the GNS3 settings file ~/.gns3/gns3.ini (OS X/Linux) or %APPDATA%\gns3.ini (Windows). If it does not exist, it runs the **Setup Wizard**. If the **Setup Wizard** did not run, quit GNS3, delete this file and run GNS3 again.

The process is similar for each operating system, and the Windows setup is shown here, with references to the other operating systems as needed.

Warning: Double check that you completed that important pre-installation prerequisite and already have a router image in your Images directory, otherwise you won't be able to complete all the steps that the **Setup Wizard** will take you through.

The setup wizard

This is the most important part of the installation, and the most daunting! Don't give up, I'll help you through it.

The first step is to **configure the path to your OS images (IOS, Qemu, PIX etc.) directory**. Remember, you copied your images to your `%HOMEPATH%\GNS3\Images` directory before you began the install. (Or your `~/GNS3/Images` directory).

Click on the number **1** to bring up the GNS3 **Preferences** dialogue for **General Settings**. Note that the **OS images (IOS, Qemu, PIX etc.)** directory is set to the directory where you copied your images. If this is not correct, change it now. Also note that there is a **Projects directory**. It should be set to be located on the same `GNS3` directory branch as your **OS images (IOS, Qemu, PIX etc.)** directory.

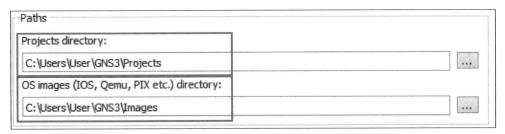

Click on **OK** and you will be asked if you want to **create the project and image directories**. Click on **Yes** to have GNS3 create the `Projects` directory for you.

Back at the **Setup Wizard**, click on the number **2** to bring up the GNS3 **Preferences** dialogue for **Dynamips**. The key point here is to click on the **Test Settings** button. This is to verify that the path to Dynamips is correct. If you do NOT see a message like **Dynamips 0.2.10 successfully started**, then you will need to troubleshoot. The most likely cause is that the path to Dynamips is incorrect or Dynamips was not installed correctly.

Click on **OK** to dismiss the **Preferences** dialogue and return to the **Setup Wizard** where you will now click on the number **3**. This will open the **IOS images and hypervisors** dialogue.

This is the dialogue where you tell GNS3 which of the IOS images you copied to your `Images` directory you wish to use. The process is a little tricky, so use the next diagram for help.

Step 1: Select an image file

Click on the ellipsis **(...)** next to the **Image file** prompt. A file browser will open at your Images directory. Select an IOS image and click on **OK**. If the image is compressed (which is likely if this is the first image you have selected), then you will be presented with a dialogue asking if you would like to uncompress it. Some images simply won't work unless they have been decompressed, and it is always a good idea to "uncompress" the image anyway because your simulated routers will load much faster.

By convention, compressed images use a .bin extension, and uncompressed images use a .image extension.

Don't stop. Your image isn't added yet!

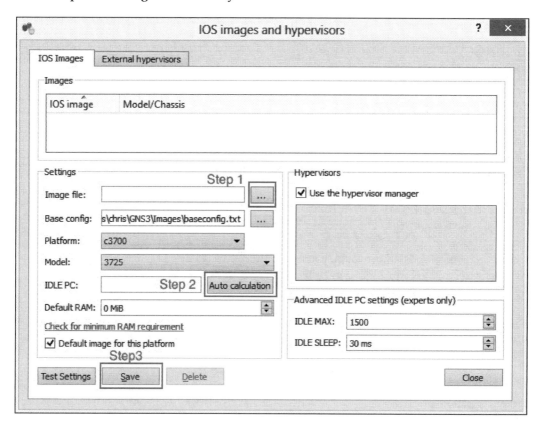

Step 2: Configure the Idle-PC value

There have been many tears wept, many heads banged and many disappointments suffered by people who neglect this rather inelegant feature. The actual reason for an Idle-PC value, and what is does, is discussed in *Chapter 2, Creating your First GNS3 Simulation*. For now, just be happy that since GNS3 0.8.4, there is an easy way to **Auto calculate** the Idle-PC value – possibly saving you hours of searching for a good value. Without an Idle-PC value, your routers will potentially run your computer's CPU to 100 percent.

I suggest you open your **Windows Task Manager** (or run `top` in a terminal window on OS X/Linux) before you commence this process so you can observe the CPU usage as GNS3 attempts to find an Idle-PC value.

 Warning: During this step your computer is likely to become unresponsive at times. Make sure your computer is not busy with other important tasks during this step.

Click on the **Auto Calculation** button for the Idle-PC value. A progress dialogue will appear. Don't be alarmed if your computer's CPU jumps to 100 percent several times during this process, or even if you see **Application Not Responding** messages.

If GNS3 is not able to find a good Idle-PC value, you will see a **Failed to find a working Idle PC value** message. Before you try again, make sure you have absolutely all other applications on your computer closed (except perhaps **Windows Task Manager**), and try again. When the process is finished, close the dialogue.

Optionally, you can now click on the **Test Settings** button, which simply boots your router image so you can check your CPU usage. If your CPU usage is still high, make a note of the previously allocated Idle-PC value, and try again.

Don't stop. Your image may not be added yet!

Step 3: Save your settings

If you used the **Auto calculation**, then GNS3 would have saved your configuration automatically, but if you manually typed your own Idle-PC or left it blank, then you need to click on **Save** before your settings are saved for this image. If you try to add another image before saving, you will simply overwrite the one you have already selected.

Unfortunately, there is no warning if you click on **Close** without saving. The best you can do is look at the list of images at the top of the window. If your image is not listed there, then you can be sure it has not been saved.

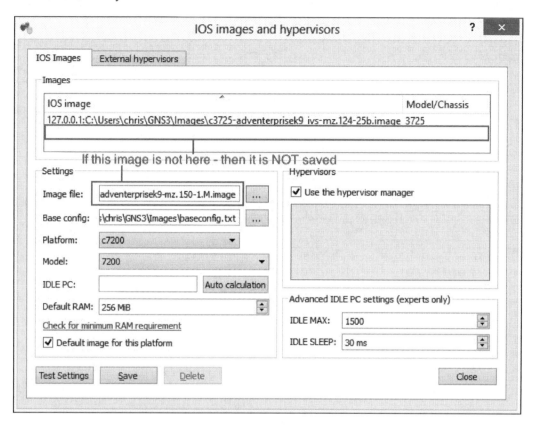

Step 4: Check the base config

GNS3 makes every effort to try and make things easy for you, but some features do so at the expense of making the GNS3 simulation less like a real hardware router.

The **Base config** is such a feature.

When you boot a hardware router for the first time, you are greeted at the console with a message:

```
        --- System Configuration Dialog ---
Would you like to enter the initial configuration dialog? [yes/no]:
```

But if you have a **Base config** file specified, GNS3 boots the router with the configuration from that file applied which is a great time saver and even assists in keeping your CPU under control if you have a lot of routers. (Having a lot of routers sitting at the [yes/no] prompt can spike your CPU).

You can edit the baseconfig.txt file if you wish to customize it, or even have a different file for each router image. By default, it is found in your Images directory.

Or if you want your simulations to be more "real-world" and boot to the System Configuration Dialog, and the [yes/no] prompt then you can delete this setting, leaving it blank. But don't forget to click on **Save** again after deleting the field.

Summary

In this chapter you have learned about the GNS3 family of applications, and hopefully now have a better appreciation of the many contributors to this product.

You now know how as to work out if your computer is going to be powerful enough to handle the size of the simulations you wish to run.

You have followed the process of downloading the appropriate files for your installation and installing them in the recommended order, and gone through the essential installation steps of defining the images and projects directories, tested your Dynamips installation and configured at least one IOS image ready for inclusion in a simulation. Ideally, you will have found a good Idle-PC value for this image, and you now have a working installation of GNS3 ready to build your first GNS3 project with Cisco emulated routers and the Virtual PC Simulator, which is of course what you will be doing in the next chapter.

2
Creating your First GNS3 Simulation

Even if you have used GNS3 before, there are some important background concepts covered in this chapter that will help you get the most out of GNS3.

The following topics will be covered in this chapter:

- Jumping in the deep end – a basic two-router configuration
- Conceptualizing a project
- Getting to know the GUI
- Using VPCS (Virtual PC Simulator)
- Capturing packets with Wireshark
- Avoiding the 100 percent CPU utilization problem
  - Getting to grips with Idle-PC values
- Introducing the GNS3 generic switches

After reading this chapter, you will have a better understanding of how you will be able to use basic GNS3 features most effectively.

This chapter assumes you have at least a very basic understanding of the Cisco router configuration, but even if you don't, if you follow the instructions you will be able to complete the exercises.

Jumping in the deep end – a basic two-router configuration

If you have completed all of the setup steps from *Chapter 1, Clearing the First Hurdle*, start by opening GNS3 and following the enlisted steps. If you haven't completed your setup, then don't try this yet.

Step 1: Open the workspace

If you have just launched GNS3, you will see the **New Project** dialogue box opened. If you already have GNS3 opened, navigate to **File | New Blank Project** to reach the **New Project** dialogue box. In the **Project Name:** field, type *Basic2Routers*, or some other name of your choice. Note that as you type the name of your project, the name of the project directory is filled in for you automatically.

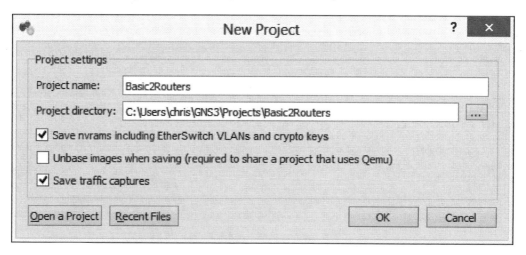

Check the **Save nvrams including EtherSwitch VLANs and crypto keys** option. Normally you would leave this option **unchecked**, but you will see the effect this has in the following section. Also **check** the **Save traffic captures** option. Leave the **Unbase images…** option **unchecked**.

Now click on **OK** to start your project. The main workspace screen will open with your project name in the GNS3 window **Title Bar**. I have labeled several other parts of the entire GNS3 Windows for later reference in the following diagram:

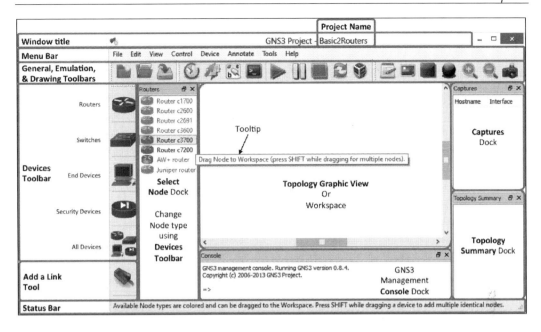

Note particularly the **Devices Toolbar**, the main **Topology Graphic View** or area **Workspace**, the docking windows for the **GNS3 Management Console**, and the **Topology Summary**. You can see the names of each of the areas and other tooltips by hovering the mouse cursor over the area. Note that you will often see additional information in the **Status Bar** area as well. You won't see the **Routers** dock until the next step.

Step 2: Add routers to your topology

Click on the **Router** icon in the **Devices Toolbar** (on the left hand side of your screen), and you will see the **Routers** dock appear, showing the routers supported by GNS3. These icons will be greyed out unless you have an image of a particular router type. You can see in the preceding figure that this installation has router images for both the Cisco c3700 and c7200 series router.

As always, I will assume that you have an image for a c3700 router—but the following exercises could just as easily be conducted with any other model equipped with at least two FastEthernet interfaces by default, such as a c2621.

Click on the **Router c3700** icon and drag it onto the workspace. The first time you do this, *Dynamips* will start up and you may notice a delay of a couple of seconds before the image drops and a router called **R1** appears.

You can hold down the <*Shift*> key as you drag the router icon into the workspace and you will presented with a dialog box allowing you to drop multiple routers into the workspace in a straight line or a circular fashion.

Now repeat the process, dragging another c3700 router across so that you have two routers in your workspace. Notice how the second router (**R2**) dropped onto the workspace more quickly because *Dynamips* is already running. Your workspace should now look something like the following figure:

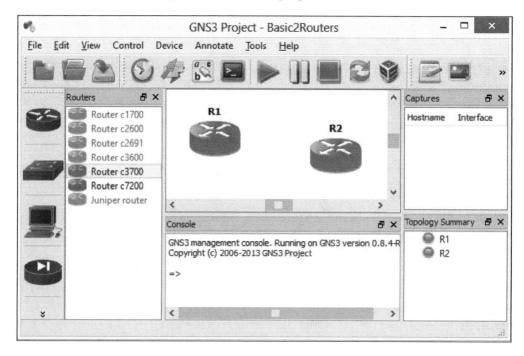

Step 3: Connect the routers together

To do this, click on the **Add a link** tool in the left hand pane (If a pop-up menu appears, choose **FastEthernet**). The icon will change to include a white-on-red X to indicate that the **Add a link** tool is active, and you cursor will change to a + shape.

Click your cursor on one router, select the **f0/0** interface, then click on the other router and again select the **f0/0** interface. You can now either hit the *<Esc>* key or click on the now modified **Add a link** icon 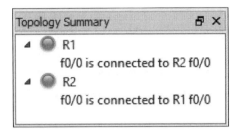 to get your normal cursor back.

You will now have connected the two router interfaces. If you don't see the red connection status indicators (the two little red dots on the link between the routers) then move your routers a little further apart until they appear.

It is almost time to configure the routers, but before you do, take a look at the **Topology Summary** in the bottom right hand pane. Click on each of the triangular icons next to the router names (**R1** and **R2**) and you will see a summary of the connections you just completed.

Topology Summary

> R1
>   f0/0 is connected to R2 f0/0
> R2
>   f0/0 is connected to R1 f0/0

Step 4: Start your routers

Navigate to **Control | Start/Resume all devices** (or click on the green **Start/Resume all devices** icon in the toolbar—also known as the "**Play**" button). After some time (it may be several seconds), your connection indicators on the link between the two routers should turn green, and the **Status Indicators** next to the router names in your **Topology Summary** list should also turn green.

Step 5: Configure your routers

Now that the routers are running, navigate to **Control | Console connect to all devices**, and your terminal application should open windows or tabs to each of your routers. The following figure is taken from GNS3 running on Windows that has been configured to use *SuperPutty* as the terminal application. Other terminal applications are discussed in *Chapter 3, Enhancing GNS3*.

Troubleshooting: If your terminal application doesn't open, go to GNS3 **Preferences** (by navigating to **Edit | Preferences** on Windows or **GNS3 | Preferences** on OS X) at the **General** settings and click on the **Terminal** tab. Check that the command in the **Terminal command:** field is valid for your installation. For help read the *Terminal Tips* section in *Chapter 3, Enhancing GNS3*.

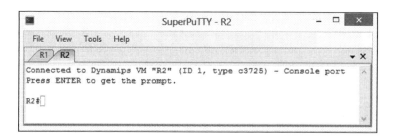

Notice that SuperPutty has two tabs labeled **R1** and **R2**. Other terminal applications will have something similar, or may open two separate windows. Simply click on the tab/window of the router you wish to configure.

If you only want to open the console to a single router, you can simply double-click on the router icon. If the router is running, the console will open. (If the router is not running, the **Node configurator** dialog box will open).

However, be careful that you don't get carried away double-clicking, or else you may find that you have multiple sessions to the same router!

SuperPutty troubleshooting: I have found that SuperPutty doesn't always open console connections to all routers. If you see only one router opened, return to the main GNS3 window and double-click on the router that doesn't have a console opened yet.

For this exercise, configure the **f0/0** interface of each router on the same subnet and bring the interfaces up as follows — just type the commands as you see them (the commands are the words written in *italics*):

On router R1

R1#configure terminal

R1(config)#interface f0/0

R1(config-if)#ip address 10.0.0.1 255.255.255.0

R1(config-if)#no shutdown

R1(config-if)#end

The commands to configure router R2 are exactly the same, except we use the IP address 10.0.0.2 on interface **f0/0**. When completed, ping the other router using the following command line:

R2#ping 10.0.0.1

If you didn't make any mistakes, you should get at least some ping replies (you rarely get 100 percent ping replies the first time you send a ping, because of the time the ARP process takes to complete).

Congratulations—you have built your first working simulation. But of course you will want to save this masterpiece.

Step 6: Save your configuration

Saving your configuration is NOT a single action process. There is more than one thing to save, firstly your router configurations must be saved within the emulated router environment itself, and the GNS3 configuration (the types of routers in your topology, their position on the workspace and so on) also needs to be saved.

Start by saving the configurations on each of your routers with the *write memory* command (or the *copy running-config startup-config* command if you prefer) as in the following command:

Rx#write memory

Next, back in the GNS3 main window, navigate to **File | Save Project** and your project will be saved in the directory indicated when you created the project. If you didn't name a project back in *Step 1* then GNS3 will stop your devices (after warning you) before the save takes place.

> Before you save your project, make sure your **Topology Graphic View** window is showing all your devices, because GNS3 automatically takes a screenshot as you save and place a file called topology.png in your chosen Project_Name directory.

In the following section, you will explore exactly what files make up a **Project** like the one you just saved.

Conceptualizing a project

The project you just created and saved was saved as a collection of files and folders. In this section, you will explore those files and where they live.

Use a file browser to browse to the location of your GNS3 `Projects` directory (typically on Windows this is `%HOMEPATH%\GNS3\Projects`; on OS X and Linux this is `~/GNS3/Projects`). You should find, a directory there with the same name as the project you just created. Open that directory and you will see your `topology.net` file, a `topology.png` file, and four directories called `captures`, `configs`, `qemu-flash-drives`, and `working`. If you had not **checked** the **Save nvrams including EtherSwitch VLANs and crypto keys** option when you created your project, you would not see the `working` directory.

 Some operating systems like to confuse users by hiding the `".net"` and `".png"` part of the filename, so you may see the `topology.net` and the `topology.png` files both listed simply as **"topology"**.

The `captures` directory will hold the Wireshark packet captures. Wireshark is discussed under the heading *Capturing Packets with Wireshark* later in the chapter. The `qemu-flash-drives` directory will be discussed in *Chapter 4, Unleashing Other Emulators*.

The topology.net file

Take a look at the `topology.net` file in a text editor. The inner workings of this file are discussed in *Chapter 5, The Cisco Connection*, but for now, notice that there is a section in this file for each of the routers (**R1** and **R2**) and within each section is a reference to the location of the startup configuration file for the router given on the line that reads for example, `cnfg = configs\R1.cfg`.

Notice also that there is a line in each section that shows that the **f0/0** interface of each router is connected to the other — the lines that read for example `f0/0 = R1 f0/0`.

The configs directory

Back in your file browser, browse to the `configs` directory of your project. Notice that there are two files there, `R1.cfg` and `R2.cfg`. Again using a text editor, examine these files and you will see that they contain the startup configuration as was saved when you issued the *write memory* command. The `configs` directory is also used to store any **VPCS** configuration files you save (VPCS is discussed later in the *Using VPCS (Virtual PC Simulator)* section).

The working directory

Finally, take a look at the `working` directory. If you hadn't checked the **Save nvrams including EtherSwitch VLANs and crypto keys** option when you started the project, this directory wouldn't be here.

Normally, saving the `working` directory is not necessary; however there are some cases where it is necessary to save the `working` directory. These are as follows:

- When you have any VLAN configuration on your router
- When you have generated keys for ssh or AAA

At other times, saving the working directory only consumes additional disk space.

Having now explored the file collection that is created when saving a project, you should make sure you know how to open a project. It is actually not quite the reverse of saving.

Opening a project

Navigate to **File | Open Project**. You will be presented with the **Open a file** dialog box browsing your `Projects` directory—but unlike when you named your project, selecting the directory with the name of your project is not quite enough—you will have to then go one step further and find the `topolgogy.net` file that was saved along with your project. There are long and convoluted reasons why this works this way, but it doesn't take much imagination to realize that you could actually edit the `topology.net` file in a text editor and save is say as `new_topology.net` and have both variations sitting in this directory.

By default, GNS3 searches for *.net files to open. If you change the search criteria in the **Open a file** dialog box to **All files** or *.*, you will also be able to see the topology.png screenshot file that was saved when saved your project. If you have your file browser set to allow file preview, you can take a look at the topology.png file and even choose the topology.png to open.

For now, find the topology.net for the *Basic2Routers* project you completed earlier, and open it. You will use this topology as you explore the Graphical User Interface in the next section.

Getting to know the GUI

Your screen should look like it did when you saved your project. You will have to admit that it is very basic. In this section, you will add some text and align the objects to get your topology to look very neat, but first you should become familiar with the basic toolbar set, which consists of a **General**, an **Emulation**, and a **Drawing** toolbar located across the top of your screen. If you hover your mouse over each tool, in turn you will discover there are tools for **New Blank Project, Open Project or topology file, Save Project, Manage Snapshots, Import/Export IOS Startup Configs, Show/ Hide interface labels, Start Console..., Start/Resume all devices, Suspend all devices, Stop all devices, Reload all devices, Show VirtualBox Manager, Reload all devices, Add a note, Insert a picture, Draw a rectangle, Draw an ellipse, Zoom in, Zoom out**, and **Take a screenshot**. However, wherever possible I will refer to the equivalent menu items, in case you have hidden any of the toolbars.

Step 1: Add Text

One of the most useful and under-used tools in GNS3 is the text box. With your *Basic2Routers* project opened, navigate to **Annotate | Add note**. Your cursor changes to a cross-hair.

Now click somewhere on the workspace, and type *10.0.0.0/24* to document the subnet you created between R1 and R2. When you have finished typing, click on another spot in the workspace and your cursor will turn to an arrow.

Finally, use the arrow cursor to pick up the text you just entered and move it to sit between your two routers. Your workspace should now look something like the following image:

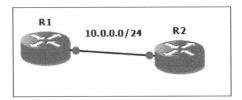

There is also a handy feature in the **File** menu — **Screenshot**, which I used to capture the preceding figure.

Step 2: Align objects

Like me, you probably don't have your routers perfectly aligned. GNS3 has an easy way of lining them up.

Select the objects you wish to align. (Click-and-drag in the workspace or click on one of the objects then press *<Shift>* and click on each of the other objects).

The selected objects will change color to be slightly darker, or in the case of text boxes and graphic objects, will be outlined by a dotted line.

There is a **Draw a rectangle when an item is selected** option in GNS3 **Preferences** in the **General** settings under the **GUI Settings** tab that you can check, which makes it easier to tell if an object is selected or not.

Now, with the objects selected that you wish to align, navigate to **Device | Align horizontally** (or right-click on the workspace to get the **Device** menu) and your objects will align. As you can see, there is also an option to **Align vertically** as well.

Tips for managing your workspace

- By now you have probably discovered that moving the mouse wheel up/ down and left/right moves the workspace around. You can also use the arrow keys on your keyboard to achieve the same effect.
- If you hold the *<Ctrl>* key while you move your mouse wheel up/down, the workspace will zoom in and out.
  - The option **Zoom using Mouse Wheel** from **View** reverses the action of both the above

- You can click and drag the device name (**R1** or **R2**) to another part of the screen such as under the device or on top of the device if you like.

- If you navigate to **View | Show interface labels**, (or use the **Show interface labels** tool from the toolbar) then you are likely to want to move these labels around—but if you move devices around later, it is very easy to end up with interface labels in the wrong places. Thankfully, there is a **Reset interface labels** option under **View**, but you will have to toggle the **Show interface labels** setting from **View** before you can use it.

Tips for managing your routers

- Normally you configure your routers using console access. However, it is actually possible to change the `startup-config` of a router before you run it (provided it has been saved at least once). Just select the router and navigate to **Device | Startup-config** and you will be able to edit the `startup-config` directly.

- If you were working with real hardware and you wished to reload a router's configuration, you could either turn off the power, or use the Cisco IOS `reload` command. Unfortunately, *Dynamips* is not able to detect if you use this command, and if you try, your console will become inoperative. Luckily there is a work-around—if you ever need to reload a router, select the router and navigate to **Device | Reload**. Or you can right-click on a device to activate the **Device** menu.

- If you want to leave your computer but don't want to stop your routers, press the **Suspend all devices** tool on the toolbar to save CPU cycles and of course save energy. It is especially important if you are running on battery power.

Using VPCS (Virtual PC Simulator)

One of the most frustrating features of working in a simulated environment is generating test traffic to pass though your simulated network. The job of generating test traffic is where the little application VPCS (Virtual PC Simulator) comes into its own.

VPCS is a lightweight application that can simulate up to nine computers from a single command line interface. From the command line you can ping and traceroute to GNS3 devices, and even send streams of UDP and TCP packets if you wish.

In this section, I will show you how to use VPCS in your GNS3 environment to expand your network to look like the following figure.

Step 1: Add host devices to your topology

Start by opening GNS3 and loading the *Basic2Routers* project you created earlier.

Now click on the **End Devices** icon (looks like a computer) the in the **Devices Toolbar** (on the left hand side of your screen). Next, click on the **Host** icon and while holding the <*Shift*> key, drag the icon into your workspace and when prompted, tell GNS3 that you need two of these devices.

Arrange the device icons so that they sit under your routers. You are about to connect one VPC to each router.

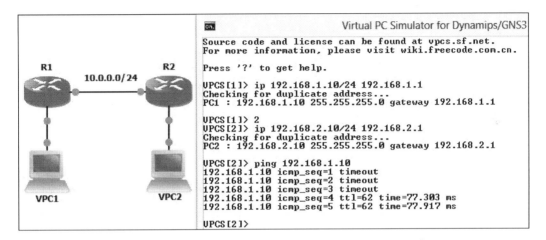

Step 2: Rename you VPCs

Using your mouse, select **both** the VPC icons, and then navigate to **Device | Change the hostname**. Rename **C1** to *VPC1* and **C2** to *VPC2*.

Step 3: Connect your VPCS to your routers

Switch to the **Add a link** tool and click on **VPC1**. By default, the **computer** type cloud icon is allocated an interface for every interface on your host computer, plus nine more which are ready to use with **VPCS**. The interface you need for VPC1 is the first **NIO_UDP** interface, labeled **nio_upd:30000:127.0.0.1:20000**. Select it and link it to **R1 f0/1**. Repeat the process to link the second NIO_UDP interface — **nio_udp:30001:127.0.0.1:20001** on **VPC2** to **R2 f0/1**.

This linking process modifies your configuration to tell *Dynamips* that, firstly, it is to listen on UDP ports 30000 and 30001 and secondly, it should say router R1 attempt to forward a packet of any kind out of interface **f0/1**, *Dynamips* is to take the entire Ethernet frame and put it in the payload of a UDP packet, and send it to 127.0.0.1:20001 which is of course where the VPCS will be listening for packets.

Step 4: Start the VPCS application

Navigate to **Tools | VPCS** to open a VPCS command window. If you see a **Windows Security Alert**, click on **Allow access**.

By default, your VPCS application will open with no VPCS configured and the prompt showing VPCS[1]. If your prompt looks different, then type the digit 1 at the command prompt and hit *<Enter>* to bring VPC1 into focus.

To build the topology shown earlier, VPC1 will need an IP address of 192.168.1.10/24 and a default gateway of 192.168.1.1, and VPC2 will need an IP address of 192.168.2.10/24 and a default gateway of 192.168.2.1. Typing the following commands into the VPCS command interface will achieve this. Remember; only enter the commands shown in *italics*.

```
VPCS[1] > ip 192.168.1.10/24 192.168.1.1
Checking for duplicate address...
PC1 : 192.168.1.10 255.255.255.0 gateway 192.168.1.1
```

To change focus to VPC2, type the number 2 and hit *<Enter>*, then configure the IP using the following commands:

```
VPCS[1] > 2
VPCS[2] > ip 192.168.2.10/24 192.168.2.1
Checking for duplicate address...
computer2 : 192.168.2.10 255.255.255.0 gateway 192.168.2.1
```

Check your configuration with the *show ip* and *show ip all* commands shown as follows:

```
VPCS[2] > show ip
NAME        : VPCS[2]
IP/MASK     : 192.168.2.10/24
GATEWAY     : 192.168.2.1
DNS         :
MAC         : 00:50:79:66:68:01
```

```
LPORT       : 20001
RHOST:PORT  : 127.0.0.1:30001
MTU:        : 1500
```

VPCS[2] > *show ip all*

```
NAME    IP/MASK                GATEWAY          MAC                    DNS
VPCS1   192.168.1.10/24        192.168.1.1      00:50:79:66:68:00
VPCS2   192.168.2.10/24        192.168.2.1      00:50:79:66:68:01
<...output omitted...>
```

 Note that for VPCS[2], the show ip command shows that VPCS is listening for packets on UDP port 20001, and should VPCS[2] ever send a frame, it will encapsulate the whole frame, and forward it to 127.0.0.1:30001.

Of course, you can't expect to be able to send frames to and from VPCS to the routers, until the routers have some IP addresses on appropriate interfaces.

Step 5: Configure your routers

To configure your routers to match the IP addressing for your VPCS, you will need to configure interface **f0/1** on **R1** with an IP address of 192.168.1.1/24 and interface **f0/1** on **R2** with an IP address of 192.168.2.1/24. I'm sure you will also want to have your network so VPC1 can ping VPC2, so you will need to configure routing on your routers. For the purpose of this exercise, you will configure OSPF routing using the lazy configuration (*network 0.0.0.0 255.255.255.255 area 0*) for OSPF.

Make sure you have your routers started and the console window opened. The following commands are used to configure the routers:

On router R1

R1#*configure terminal*
R1(config)#*interface f0/1*
R1(config-if)#*ip address 192.168.1.1 255.255.255.0*
R1(config-if)#*no shutdown*
R1(config-if)#*exit*
R1(config)#*router ospf 1*
R1(config-router)#*network 0.0.0.0 255.255.255.255 area 0*
R1(config-router)#*end*
R1#ping *192.168.1.10*

If you get replies from your ping, then your connection between the router and the VPCS is working just fine.

The commands to configure router **R2** are exactly the same, except use the IP address of **192.168.2.1** on interface **f0/1**.

From your VPCS console, you should be able to ping the other VPC using the following command:

```
VPCS[2]> ping 192.168.1.10
192.168.1.10 icmp_seq=1 timeout
192.168.1.10 icmp_seq=2 ttl=62 time=77.770 ms
```

VPCS is an extremely handy troubleshooting tool. Before continuing, you should try the following commands in your VPCS command window:

help

show

show arp

ping ?

ping 192.168.1.10 –P 17

ping 192.168.1.10 –P 6

trace ?

trace 192.168.1.10

Step 6: Save and cleanup

Recall that on each router you have to enter the command *write memory* in privileged mode, and that from GNS3, navigate to **File | Save project** to properly save a project—but unfortunately that does not save your VPCS configuration. To do that, go to the VPCS command window and issue the command *save startup.vpc* as follows:

VPCS [1] > *save startup.vpc*

This will save a copy of your current configuration in the file called `startup.vpc` in your project's `configs` directory. As the name suggests, it will automatically load the next time you open this project and launch VPCS.

You can save files under any name, and load them later with the *load <filename>* command. They are simply text files which you can edit in a text editor if you wish, and even include extra commands such as `set echo off` and `echo <text>` to create a script file to say, test a configuration for completeness.

Now quit VPCS with the *quit* command, as the following:

VPCS[1] > *quit*

As VPCS quits, it saves a copy of your command history in a text file called `vpcs.hist` in your project's `configs` directory so your command history will still be available the next time you load the project.

If you quit GNS3 before quitting VPCS, VPCS will still keep running. This means that if you restart GNS3, and try and start VPCS again, you will get errors. Therefore you must remember to always quit VPCS using the *quit* command.

As a final exercise, you should now make sure your **router** configurations are saved (using the *write memory* command), and that your **GNS3 project** is saved (by navigating to **File | Save project**), and quit GNS3. Then restart GNS3, reload your project, restart your routers, launch VPCS, and check if your VPCS can still ping each other.

Capturing packets with Wireshark

Wireshark is another great tool. There is no better way to learn how protocols work than by observing them with Wireshark captures, and there is no better tool for obtaining those captures than GNS3. Together they make a great study pair. In this exercise, you will capture packets passing between the two routers in your *Basic2Routers* GNS3 project.

Step 1: Load your Basic2Routers project

Start by opening GNS3 and loading the *Basic2Routers* project you created earlier, if it is not already opened. By now your project should consist of two routers and two VPCS.

Make sure your routers are started, and open a console session to each of your routers. Make sure routing has converged on your routers using the *show ip route* and *show ip protocols* commands on your routers. If you have any problems, then check that your configuration matches the configuration shown in *Step 5: Configure your routers* in the *Jumping in the deep end - a basic two* router configuration section.

Step 2: Start the capture

The easiest way to start a capture is to right-click on one of the routers to bring up the **Device** menu (or select a router and click on the **Device** menu) and select **Capture**. You will be prompted to select an interface to start the capture on. Since you want to capture the OSPF packets between the routers, click on the **f0/0** interface.

Look at the **Captures** dock and your recently started capture should be listed there. Now right-click on your capture and select **Start Wireshark**. Note that you also have the option of stopping your capture. If you do stop the capture, the **Captures** dock stays there, and the **capture indicator** turns from green to red, allowing you to come back and re-start the capture later if you wish.

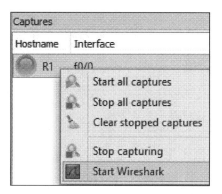

 There is an option in GNS3 **Preferences** in the **Capture** settings to **Automatically start the command when capturing**. In other words, with this option **checked**, Wireshark will automatically start each time you start a capture.

Now that you have Wireshark opened (it looks like the following figure), explore the **Filter:** prompt (1), by typing the word *ospf* at the prompt and clicking on **Apply** (2). Now you can examine the OSPF packets and dig around inside them (3).

Wireshark stores all the packets it captures in a temporary file. If you forget about this file, it can grow to consume a large amount of disk space. So it is a good idea to remember to stop your captures from within the **GNS GUI** (NOT the Wireshark GUI — that will just stop Wireshark from reading the temporary file).

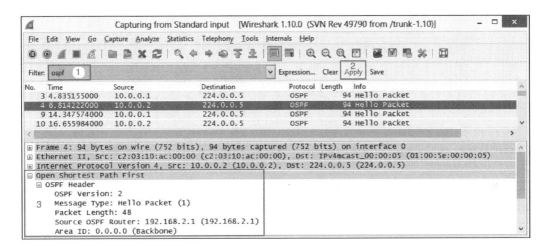

The Wireshark captures are stored either in a `captures` directory off your `Project_Name` directory if the **Save traffic captures** option was **checked** when you named the project, or in the location specified in the GNS3 **Preferences**, in the **Capture** settings under **Working directory for capture files.**

Avoiding the 100 percent CPU utilization problem

Dynamips is an emulator. It takes a binary image designed for a MIPS processor and extracts the machine code commands, just like the MIPS processor would, and tells your computer to execute the equivalent command on your Intel or AMD processor. But many of these instructions will simply be code, to tell the router to wait for something to happen, such as read a packet or send some output to the console. Unfortunately, *Dynamips* doesn't know which parts of the code it is emulating are the hard working bits, and which bits are the "just hanging around" parts, so it runs them all at full pelt. 100 percent CPU utilization is the result. To prevent this 100 percent CPU utilization, you have to set an Idle-PC value. As Greg Anuzelli (the author of *Dynagen*) puts it (Anuzelli, Greg. Dynamips / Dynagen Tutorial, `http://dynagen.org/tutorial.htm` retrieved 5 Feb 2013):

> *Once [an Idle-PC value] is applied, Dynamips "sleeps" the virtual router occasionally when this idle loop is executed significantly reducing CPU consumption on the host without reducing the virtual router's capacity to perform real work.*

The 100 percent CPU utilization problem has been the Achilles heal of *Dynamips* and GNS3 forever. However, if you went through the **auto Idle-PC** process when you added your IOS images as explained in *Chapter 1, Clearing the First Hurdle*, then you may not experience this problem, but there is also a good chance that you will.

Coming to grips with Idle-PC values

Here is how to find a good Idle-PC value. Once you have found a good value for a particular image, it should be always good for that image, irrespective of the host platform you are running on. However, it is of no relevance to any other image. [The following section has been adapted from the GNS3 forum post by the author, available at http://forum.gns3.net/topic2873.html]

Step 1: Monitor your CPU

- **Windows**: Open the Windows task manager and sort by %CPU
- **Linux**: Open a terminal window and enter the command *top*
- **Mac OS X**: Open a terminal window and enter the command *top -o cpu*

Keep this window visible for the entire process.

Step 2: Prepare your router

In GNS3, start a new topology with one router ONLY and start the router.

Open the console and press <*Enter*>. When the router starts up, it sends the **Press RETURN to get started!** message, so if you don't press the <*Enter*> key, it may influence the outcome. By the same logic, if you are presented with any more prompts, press <*Ctrl*> + C to abort these.

 Many of the GNS3 terminal applications have been set up to send an <*Enter*> character as they start, so this step may not be necessary.

Step 3: Observe the CPU

Back at your task manager or console window, take note of the amount of the CPU being chewed by *Dynamips*.

Step 4: Search for an Idle-PC value

In GNS3, right-click on the router and select **Idle PC**. Answer **Yes** if warned that an **idlepc value is already applied**.

Dynamips will now make some guesses as to where a good place might be to make the program counter sit idle for a while—that is an **Idle Program Counter (Idle-PC)** location. While this is happening, your CPU will probably run close to 100 percent.

A list of **possible idlepc values** should appear, hopefully at least one of them will be marked with an asterisk (*). If no values appear marked with *, try again.

When you find a value marked with a *, write it down. If multiple values appear with *, write them all down (in a column) before choosing each one of them in turn and clicking on **Apply**.

Step 5: Choose the best Idle-PC value

Check the CPU utilization for *Dynamips* in the task manager or console window for each Idle-PC value you find.

Estimate the average CPU consumption for *Dynamips* over say 15-20 seconds and write it down next to the Idle-PC value you wrote down in the last step.

If you have an Idle-PC value that shows less than 10-15 percent CPU, you may want to go to the next step, else, go back to *Step 4*.

Step 6: Check that your Idle-PC value is recorded

Navigate to **Edit | IOS images and hypervisors**. Select the image you are using and check the **IDLE PC** value—it should match the last value tested. If you went through the process multiple times and feel that one of your earlier attempts was a better value, then record that value here and GNS3 will automatically use that value in any new topologies you create, and modify any topology you load using this model router (don't forget to click on **Save**).

You will also see options here for **IDLE-MAX** and **IDLE-SLEEP**. These are also related to the Idle-PC value. Dynamips doesn't go to sleep every time the program counter hits the Idle-PC. It waits until it has hit the **Idle-PC Idle-Max** times before sleeping for **Idle-Sleep** milliseconds. That way the router still gets a chance to do the things it needs to do between visits to the Idle-PC value. If you adjust the **Idle-Max** too low or the **Idle-Sleep** too high, your emulated routers will slow down to a crawl, they will lose connections with their neighbors and bad things will happen.

Introducing GNS3 generic switches

At some time you will need to connect multiple routers together, as you would on a physical Ethernet switch or a WAN switch such as a frame-relay or an ATM switch. You could use additional router nodes to perform these functions, but in an effort to provide this functionality with much less resource usage, *Dynamips* (and hence GNS3) created its own range of virtual devices that do an excellent job of providing virtual connections between devices.

This section will show you not only how to add a generic Ethernet switch, but also how to add additional interfaces to your routers using two different methods —manual and automatic.

Ethernet switch

Probably the most useful of these switches will be the Ethernet switch. You will get to explore this in more detail in *Chapter 3, Enhancing GNS3*. In this exercise, you will add two switches, and connect each of your routers to each of the switches, and at the same time add an extra line card to your routers to be able to achieve this. The final topology you are aiming for looks like the following figure:

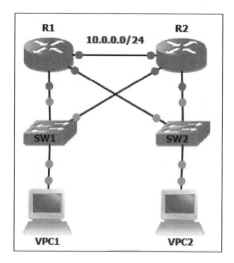

Step 1: Remove links to VPCS

In GNS3, open your *Basic2Routers* topology. You are about to add switches between your routers and VPCS, so start by right-clicking on the links (aim for the connection indicator dots if they are visible) between the routers and VPCS and selecting **Delete**.

> If you find it too hard to right-click on the link within the workspace, you can locate the link in the **Topology Summary** and right-click on it there.

Step 2: Add Ethernet switches

Click on the **Switches** tool on the left hand toolbar. Select **Ethernet switch** and add two of them to your topology between the routers and the VPCS. The idea is that you will connect each router to each switch, and connect your VPCS computers to the switches.

But if you are to connect each router to each switch, you have a problem. The routers you have in your topology only have two Ethernet interfaces, and you have used one of them to connect one router to the other router. Before you can connect each router to **both** your Ethernet switches, you will have to add another Ethernet interface to each router.

Step 3: Add an interface to your routers

Before you add interfaces to the routers, it is best to ensure that they are powered down first, so if your routers are running, use the **Stop all devices** option from **Control** now.

Select both your routers and navigate to **Device | Configure**. The **Node configurator** window will open. Click on the **Router** icon in the left hand pane labeled **Routers c3700** (1, in the following figure). Note that the right-hand pane heading now reads **Routers c3700 group**. This means that it is possible to add configuration items to the whole group at once, which is what you are about to do.

Click on the **Slots** tab (2). You should notice that **slot 1** is empty. Click on the drop-down menu for **slot 1** (3) and select **NM-1FE-TX** (4). Then click on **Apply**.

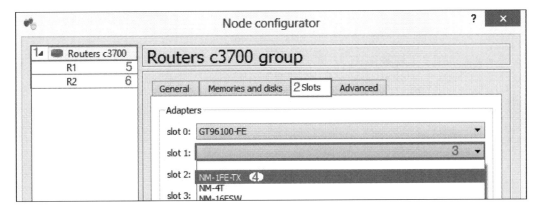

Before you click on **OK** you should check that the NM-FE-1TX module has indeed been added to R1 and R2 by clicking on R1 and R2 individually.

 You can get GNS3 to automatically add appropriate modules to your routers by holding the <*Shift*> key when you select the **Add a link** tool and select the type of link you wish to use. When you now click on a router, it will automatically add a module of the correct type and connect to the first port of that module.

Step 4: Connect your new interfaces to the switches

Now use the **Add a link** tool to connect **R1 f0/1** to **SW1** port **1**, and **R1 f1/0** to **SW2** port **1**. Notice that each switch has 8 ports. Continue by connecting **R2 f0/1** to **SW1** port **2**, and **R2 f1/0** to **SW2** port **2**. Finally, re-connect your VPCS to port **3** of their respective switches.

You can cancel the **Add a link** tool by pressing the <*Esc*> key. Your topology should now look like the figure shown before *Step 1*.

Step 5: Observe switch configuration

By default, the generic switch devices that you just added have all ports configured in VLAN 1, just like most commercial switches. However, before you finish this stage, you should check out the switch port/VLAN configuration. You will explore the VLAN configuration in more detail in *Chapter 3, Enhancing GNS3*.

Select one of the switches and select **Configure** from the **Device** menu. Click on the switch name in the left-hand pane. Notice that all ports are assigned to VLAN 1 and are of type access.

If you double-click on a particular port, it brings that port into focus so that you can edit the settings if you desire. In the following figure port 3 has been brought into focus by this method.

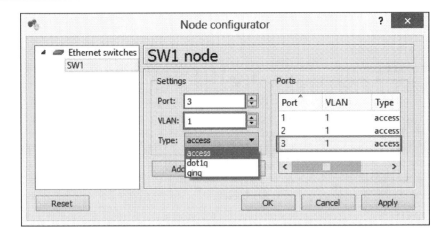

Before leaving this screen, note that in the **Type:** field, there are options to change the port type to **dot1q** or **qinq**.

And finally, once you save your configuration and reload it, if you return to the preceding screen, expect that your switch will have lost some ports, because GNS3 only record the ports that have been used when you execute the save—however, new ports will be automatically added should you ever need them.

Frame-relay and ATM switches

There is not much use for frame-relay or ATM these days, but some certifications still require that you have knowledge of these technologies. Unlike the LAN Ethernet switch, Frame-relay and ATM switches need to be configured before they can be connected. The following figure shows a possible configuration for a frame-relay switch that could be used to create three virtual circuits between three routers in a fully meshed topology.

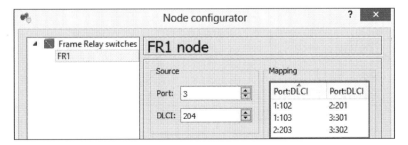

Configuring an ATM switch is similar, except of course you would configure VPIs and VCIs rather than DLCIs.

Summary

In this chapter we have explored all of the essential steps that you will need to create GNS3 topologies, including using the VPCS program to extend your simulated network to edge devices, and the Wireshark application that you can use to analyze the traffic flowing between your virtual devices. You have also learned that a GNS3 project is a collection of files and directories and you should now know how to find a suitable Idle-PC value for your images.

In the following chapter I will take you further into the capabilities of GNS3 by exploring some simple and not so simple extensions, including the somewhat tricky task of taking GNS3 outside your simulated environment and connecting it to a physical network.

3
Enhancing GNS3

In this chapter you will explore some of the more advanced features of GNS3, in particular I will be dealing with features that enhance your connectivity to and from the world outside of your GNS3 environment, as well as dealing with the more common interface enhancements that you will probably want to use.

The following topics will be covered in this chapter:

- Connecting to physical interfaces
  - Mini-project – connecting your GNS3 router to your LAN
  - The Microsoft Loopback adapter
  - The Linux NIO TAP adapter
  - The OS X TUN/TAP adapter

- Adding VLAN support
  - Generic Ethernet switch
  - EtherSwitch router

- Terminal tips
  - Using a different terminal application
  - Using the AUX port
  - Troubleshooting a device console

- Fine-tuning the topology – adding graphics and text
- Accessing GNS3 running on a remote machine
  - Accessing a device console remotely
  - Linking GNS3 topologies on different hosts

Once you have explored all the features in this chapter, you will have a simulation environment ready to build as sophisticated a Cisco router network as your hardware allows.

Connecting to physical interfaces

Now that you have created a project with virtual routers and virtual PCs, you are probably keen to find out how to connect your creations with the rest of the world via your computer's Ethernet adapter. GNS3 has a special device type designed to do just this in a variety of ways. It is the **Cloud device**.

The generic **cloud device** is presented as an **End device** in the **Devices toolbar**. There are two icons, the **Cloud** icon and the **Host** icon, which are functionally identical, you can choose whichever one suits your needs. If you just want a **Virtual Machine** (**VM**) on your host computer to be able to access the topology, you might choose a **Host** icon, but if you want your GNS3 routers to be able to access devices on your local network, you might choose the **Cloud** icon. Either way, once it is configured, the result will be the same.

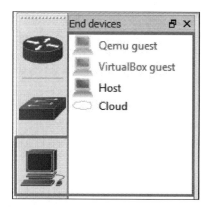

Mini-project – connecting your GNS3 router to your LAN

In some cases this is a trivial task, but host computer operating systems are tending more and more to make it difficult for applications to gain access to physical interfaces. In some cases, you may even not be able to get access to wireless interfaces. Each OS is going to have its own particular challenges, but in general you will have fewer problems if you have administrator or root access to your OS when you try to access your physical **Network Interface Card** (**NIC**).

Step 1: Connect your Ethernet NIC

This project will not work unless your Ethernet NIC is connected to a switch or other device. Make sure you know an IP address on the same subnet to which you connect your computer's NIC and verify that your host computer can ping this address. I recommend you use an Ethernet NIC rather than a wireless adapter, you may or may not have success with wireless.

Step 2: Run GNS3 as administrator/root

Linux: Run GNS3 from a terminal prompt using the command *sudo gns3&* (or *gksudo gns3&*).

OS X: Run GNS3 from a terminal prompt using the command *sudo/Applications/ GNS3.app/Contents/MacOS/GNS3*.

Windows: Right-click on your desktop shortcut to GNS3 and choose **Run as administrator**. Alternatively, open a command prompt as administrator and enter the command *%PROGRAMFILES%\GNS3\gns3.exe*.

Step 3: Add a cloud connector to your topology

Start a new project. Add a router and a cloud device. I chose the **Cloud** icon, but the **Host** icon would have a similar result, except that the **Host** icon has all the adapters that exist on your host computer already added, so if you choose the **Host** icon you can skip the next step.

Step 4: Configure your cloud device

Select your cloud/host device. Navigate to **Device | Configure** (or simply double-click on the device). In **Node configurator**, click on your cloud device (called **C1**). The **NIO Ethernet** tab should open.

 For OS X 10.8.x (Mountain Lion), this step will not work. For an alternative method, see *The OS X TUN/TAP* adapter section in this chapter.

In the **Generic Ethernet NIO (Administrator or root access required)** interface drop-down list, you will see that GNS3 lists every adapter that it could find. Select the one that corresponds to your computer's Ethernet adapter and click on **Add**. You will see your choice added to the list of adapters that this cloud has. It is possible to add multiple adapters if you wish.

In the case of Windows, the adapter will be listed as a **Netgroup Packet Filter (NPF)** interface. The **NPF** interface comes with your **WinPcap** install, which was part of your all-in-one GNS3 install. Unfortunately, it is not obvious to most observers that the interface named something like `nio_gen_eth:\ device\npf_{6fd7f628-052c-454d-99f4-7ad3f72c0977}` is actually your Ethernet adapter and not your wireless adapter.

There is a utility on the **Tools** menu to display your **Network device list** that will help you work out which **NPF** device is actually your Ethernet adapter.

Click on **OK** to close the **Node configurator** window.

Step 5: Connect your cloud device

Use the **Add a link** tool to connect your cloud Ethernet adapter interface to one of the Ethernet interfaces (say **f0/0**) of your router, start your router, and configure the interface of the router (**f0/0**) with a spare IP address from the network your computer's Ethernet NIC is attached to. My network was `192.168.255.0/24` and I knew there was another computer attached with an IP of `192.168.255.100`, and my host computer's NIC had been assigned `192.168.255.200`. I chose `192.168.255.150/24` for the router's NIC and configured it like this:

R1#configure terminal

R1(config)#interface f0/0

R1(config-if)#ip address 192.168.255.150 255.255.255.0

R1(config-if)#no shutdown

R1(config-if)#end

Step 6: Test your connectivity

From your router, ping a device on your local network (not your host computer).

R1# ping 192.168.255.100

```
Type escape sequence to abort.
Sending 5, 100-byte ICMP Echos to 192.168.255.100, timeout is 2 seconds:
.!!!!
Success rate is 80 percent (4/5), round-trip min/avg/max = 1/9/18 ms
```

You could of course also try to ping your router from your remote device as well.

Why can't my host computer ping my router?

You already tried this, didn't you? If not, try now. Depending on your underlying operating system, it might just work (I've found it generally works on Windows XP). But if you stop and think about it for a moment, there is no reason why it should work.

Firstly, understand that the virtual routers that Dynamips emulate have two jobs to do when it comes to handling frames.

- They have to be able to read incoming frames
- They have to be able to send frames

The first task is handled by **WinPcap** on Windows and **pcap** on Linux/OS X. (Win) pcap is an application that is used by both GNS3 and Wireshark to be able to see packets that are sent to and from the host.

The second task, sending frames, is handled by the host operating system.

All frames that arrive or leave the host network adapter will be seen by (Win) pcap and will show up in a packet capture. Therefore, if any external host sends a frame to the virtual router's MAC address, (Win)pcap will see it and therefore your virtual router can also see it. If the host PC sends a frame to the virtual router's MAC address, it is also processed by (Win)pcap, so your virtual router will also see it.

So it turns out that your host computer could actually ping your router after all, except that it will never learn the MAC address of the virtual router, nor will it see any replies.

The reason for this is the way the virtual router sends frames. When the virtual router sends a frame, even if it is addressed to the host's MAC address, it is passed directly to the network interface outbound queue. There is no reason why an operating system would be looking for frames addressed to itself in the OUTBOUND queue, they arrive on an INBOUND queue.

So the end result is that the host computer can send frames to the virtual router, but the virtual router cannot send frames to the host computer, even if it has learned the correct MAC address of the host computer network interface.

Devices connected outside your local host computer (on your LAN), of course do not have this problem, so there is usually no problem communicating with them.

There are ways of making your host computer communicate with your virtual routers. But each operating system has a different approach, including adding an internal virtual bridge. If your OS is Linux or OS X, skip ahead to *The Linux NIO TAP adapter* or *The OS X TUN/TAP* adapter as appropriate.

The Microsoft Loopback adapter

The most common approach on Microsoft computer is to install a loopback adapter/interface. While running GNS3 as administrator, navigate to **Tools | Loopback Manager**. You will be presented with six options.

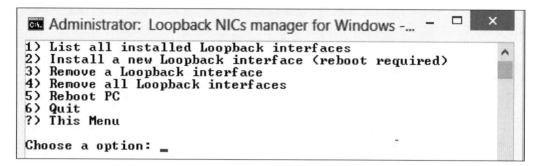

You may choose option **1) List all installed Loopback interfaces** to check that there isn't an already installed loopback interface if you wish and if not, you will need to select option **2) Install a new Loopback interface (reboot required)** before checking by selecting option **1)** again, and then finally select **5) Reboot PC**.

When your computer has rebooted, you should see an additional **Network Connection** in \Control Panel\Network and Internet\Network Connections. On my Windows 8 install, it was called **Ethernet 2**, but it might be called **Local Area Connection 2** or something similar.

Once you have given your new Windows loopback interface an IP address and default gateway address, follow **Step 2** through to **Step 6** under the *Mini-project – connecting your GNS3 router to your LAN* section using the new Loopback interface. You will of course give the router the same IP address that you used for your default gateway on your loopback interface. You will then have connectivity between your host computer and the virtual router.

The Linux NIO TAP adapter

To establish connectivity between your virtual router's interface and your host computer's interface, you will need a virtual bridge. You will also need a virtual interface to plug your router into as well. The virtual interface is the NIO TAP interface found in the uml-utilties package, and a virtual bridge can be found in the bridge-utils package. (Note: These steps rely heavily on the great information found at http://joshatterbury.com/tutorials/configuring-dynamips-to-use-a-linux-tap-interface/ and http://www.blindhog.net/linux-bridging-for-gns3-lan-communications/.)

Step 1: Install the uml-utilties and bridge-utils packages

You probably don't have these packages installed, so start by installing them by entering the following commands:

sudo apt-get update   #to be sure you have the latest

sudo apt-get install uml-utilities bridge-utils

Step 2: Create and configure the tap interface

The tap interface can be named anything you like, but in keeping with tradition, you might use **tap0**.

sudo tunctl -t tap0

ip a   #To check the tap0 interface was created

sudo ifconfig tap0 0.0.0.0 promisc up

Step 3: Create and configure the bridge

These few commands will create the bridge and add the **tap0** and **eth0** interfaces. Again, the bridge name **br0** is appropriate, but could have been something else.

sudo brctl addbr br0

sudo brctl addif br0 tap0

sudo brctl addif br0 eth0

sudo ifconfig br0 up

brctl show br0

```
bridge name  bridge id          STP enabled    interfaces
br0          8000.0050563315c6  no             eth0
                                               tap0
```

Step 4: Reassign your IP address to br0

Finally, before you can access your router, you will have to give the bridge interface br0 an IP address. If you are using DHCP:

sudo dhclient br0

Or if you are using a static IP, you'll need to assign an IP and probably a default gateway too, replacing *x*, *y*, and *z* with addresses and masks suitable for your network.

sudo ifconfig br0 x.x.x.x/y

sudo route add default gw z.z.z.z

Step 5: Configure your NIO TAP device in GNS3

While running GNS3 as root, select your cloud/host icon. Navigate to **Device |
Configure** (or simply double-click on the device). In the **Node configurator**, click on
your cloud device (called **C1**). Select the **NIO TAP** tab.

There is no drop-down list of interfaces on this tab. You will have to enter the name
tap0 as the name of your TAP interface and click on **Add** to add it to your cloud, then
click on **OK**.

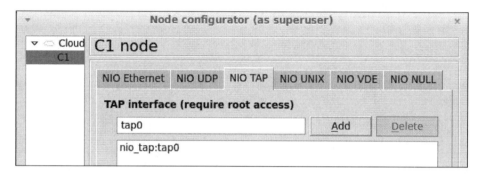

Step 6: Connect your cloud device

Use the **Add a link** tool to repeat *Step 5: Connect your cloud device* under the
Mini-project – connecting your GNS3 router to your LAN section.

Step 7: Test your connectivity

From your router, ping your host computer. My Linux host was `192.168.255.201`.

R1# *ping 192.168.255.201*

```
Type escape sequence to abort.
Sending 5, 100-byte ICMP Echos to 192.168.255.201, timeout is 2 seconds:
.!!!!
Success rate is 80 percent (4/5), round-trip min/avg/max = 2/9/28 ms
```

You could of course also try to ping your router from your host computer as well.

Step 8: Make it last

Unfortunately, most of the changes you made will be lost when you reboot. I suggest that you keep a script handy that you can run whenever you wish to use the tap interface or indeed you may even use it to launch GNS3 all the time. Here is my script, which I called `gns3tap`, and stored in `/usr/local/bin`.

```bash
#!/bin/bash
#gns3tap - a script to setup tap0 and br0 interfaces and run GNS3
#usage: sudo gns3tap
#
sudo tunctl -t tap0
sudo ifconfig tap0 0.0.0.0 promisc up
sudo brctl addbr br0
sudo brctl addif br0 tap0
sudo brctl addif br0 eth0
sudo ifconfig br0 up
sudo dhclient br0
sudo gns3
```

To create the script and make it executable:

sudo touch /usr/local/bin/gns3tap

sudo chmod +x /usr/local/bin/gns3tap

sudo pico /usr/local/bin/gns3tap

And I entered the script, and of course saved my work. To run GNS3 with the tap interface enabled, I now run:

sudo /usr/local/bin/gns3tap &

The OS X TUN/TAP adapter

The concept on Mac OS X is similar to Linux, create a tap interface and bridge to it.

Step 1: Install the TunTap package

Start by downloading the `tuntaposx` package from `http://tuntaposx.sourceforge.net`. When I did this, it came as a compressed `.tar` file that had to be decompressed until a `.pkg` file was revealed, which I installed. You can verify that the package has installed properly by running the following commands and seeing sixteen **tap** devices (**tap0 – tap15**) and sixteen **tun** devices (**tun0 – tun15**):

ls -l /dev | egrep 'tap|tun'

Step 2: Create and configure the tap interface

One of the trickiest parts of this configuration is that you do not see the **tap0** interface on your Mac until you have used it in GNS3, so this step is completed in GNS3 running as root user.

Select your cloud/host icon. Navigate to **Device | Configure** (or simply double-click on the device). In the **Node configurator**, click on your cloud device (called **C1**). Select the **NIO TAP** tab.

There is no drop-down list of interfaces on this tab. You will have to enter */dev/tap0* as the name of your TAP interface and click on **Add** to add it to your cloud, then click on **OK**.

 The device name must be */dev/tap0*, unlike the Linux **tap0**

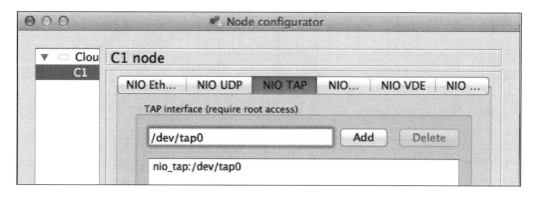

The tap interface should now be visible:

```
users-Mac:~ user$ ifconfig tap0
tap0: flags=8842<BROADCAST,RUNNING,SIMPLEX,MULTICAST> mtu 1500
    ether 9e:ce:5d:bb:c5:40
    open (pid 850)
```

Step 3: Create and configure the bridge

OS X has bridging capability built in. Here is how you create and configure it to bridge your **en0** (Ethernet interface) to your newly created **tap0** interface.

For OS X users 10.7 and earlier

Bridging was introduced with OS X 10.8 (Mountain Lion). The GNS3 forum has a "how to" for other OS X versions at `http://forum.gns3.net/topic5787.html`.

sudo ifconfig bridge0 create

sudo ifconfig bridge0 addm en0

sudo ifconfig bridge0 addm tap0

sudo ifconfig bridge0 up

ifconfig `;#To check`

Step 4: Assign an IP address to bridge0

Finally, before you can access your router, you will have to give the bridge interface **bridge0** an IP address. If you are using DHCP:

sudo ipconfig set bridge0 DHCP

Or if you are using a static IP, you'll need to assign an IP and probably a default gateway too, replacing x, y, and z with addresses and masks suitable for your network.

sudo ifconfig bridge0 x.x.x.x/y

sudo route add default gw z.z.z.z

Step 5: Test your connectivity

From your router, ping your host computer's **bridge0** IP address. In my example, my host computer (**en0**) was given a DHCP IP address of `192.168.1.75` and **bridge0** was given `192.168.1.76`.

R2#*ping 192.168.1.75*

```
Type escape sequence to abort.
Sending 5, 100-byte ICMP Echos to 192.168.1.75, timeout is 2 seconds:
.....
Success rate is 0 percent (0/5)
```

R2#*ping 192.168.1.76*

```
Type escape sequence to abort.
Sending 5, 100-byte ICMP Echos to 192.168.1.76, timeout is 2 seconds:
!!!!!
Success rate is 100 percent (5/5), round-trip min/avg/max = 4/6/9 ms
```

Note that the router was only able to ping the **bridge0** IP address, so to test connectivity in the reverse direction, you will have to tell your host Macintosh that you wish to use the **bridge0** IP address (192.168.1.76 in my case) as your source address when communicating with the router. For example (the router's IP is 192.168.1.77):

users-Mac:~ user$ *ping -S 192.168.1.76 192.168.1.77*

PING 192.168.1.77 (192.168.1.77) from 192.168.1.76: 56 data bytes

64 bytes from 192.168.1.77: icmp_seq=0 ttl=255 time=11.659 ms

The -S parameter with the ping command tells OS X to use 192.168.1.76 as the source IP when sending the pings to 192.168.1.77. For telnet, the parameter is similar, but uses a lowercase s.

users-Mac:~ user$ *telnet -s 192.168.1.76 192.168.1.77*

Trying 192.168.1.77...

Connected to 192.168.1.77.

Step 6: Make it last.

Unfortunately, like Linux, most of the changes you made will be lost when you reboot. I suggest that you keep a script handy that you can run whenever you wish to use the tap interface. Here is my script, which I called gns3tuntap and stored in a bin directory off my own home directory.

```
#!/bin/sh
#gns3tuntap - a script to setup tap0 and bridge0 interfaces
#usage: sudo ~/bin/gns3tuntap
echo Must be run AFTER the /dev/tap0 interface
echo has been created in GNS3
sudo ifconfig bridge0 create
sudo ifconfig bridge0 addm en0
sudo ifconfig bridge0 addm tap0
sudo ifconfig bridge0 up
sudo ipconfig set bridge0 DHCP
```

To create the script and make it executable:

mkdir ~/bin

touch ~/bin/gns3tuntap

chmod +x ~/bin/gns3tuntap

pico ~/bin/gns3tuntap

At this point I entered the script as preceding lines and of course saved my work. To re-enable the tap interface after I have created it in GNS3, I now run:

sudo ~/bin/gns3tuntap

Adding VLAN support

As your topologies become more sophisticated, it is certain that you will want to add VLANs to your configurations. If you are only concerned about carrying VLANs between routers, the Dynamips generic Ethernet switch does a good job. But if you want to begin practicing VLAN configuration on a simulated Cisco switch, then the closest you can get to a real switch is the EtherSwitch router.

Generic Ethernet switch

The generic Ethernet switch does not require any Cisco image and is managed completely by Dynamips, making its demand on resources far less than a Cisco device. It uses Cisco terminology to describe the port types as **access**, **dot1q**, or **qinq**.

- **Access**: These ports can be assigned to a single VLAN and accept and pass only untagged traffic.
- **Dot1q**: These ports can be assigned to a single VLAN that will be used to handle all untagged traffic, similar to the Cisco Native VLAN concept. For all other VLANs, these ports will accept and send tagged traffic.
  - To configure the untagged (native) VLAN for a **dot1q** port, firstly configure the port as an **access** port for that access VLAN, then configure it as a **dot1q** port because the **access** VLAN field becomes unavailable once the port has been designated a **dot1q** port.
- **Qinq**: These ports accept incoming frames that are already tagged and add another (outer) tag based on the access VLAN ID, as you would expect in a Q-in-Q tunnel port on a Cisco switch.

The generic switch does a reasonable job of allowing you to divide VLAN traffic between routers. However, if you need more sophistication, you could try the EtherSwitch router.

EtherSwitch router

You may have noticed that in the **Switches** dock of the **Devices toolbar**, there is an icon for an **EtherSwitch router**. This is nothing more than a Cisco 3725 router, pre-configured with a **NM-16ESW** card, which gives it 16 switch ports, quite independent from the router. The implication of this is that you must have an image for the C3725 router to be able to use the EtherSwitch device; I have found that the `c3725-adventerprisek9-mz.124-15.T10` image works well with the **EtherSwitch router** because it supports the management of VLANs without having to resort to the `vlan database` commands.

The NM-16ESW is based on older Cisco hardware and does not support many of the new switch features that CCIE and CCNP candidates are expected to learn about.

However, to overcome some of the shortcomings, there is a `baseconfig_sw.txt` file that is used as the startup configuration file for the 3725 **EtherSwitch router**. You can find this file in your `Images` directory and customize if you wish. By default it makes the following changes:

Firstly, routing is disabled. This means that if you wish to use it as a layer 3 switch, you will have to add the command *ip routing*, just like you would with say a 3750 switch. Switch ports begin at FastEthernet **1/0**, so FastEthernet **0/0** and **0/1** are shutdown and should be left shutdown if you want the device to function as a switch. Also, since these switch ports are not able to detect duplex, they have all been preconfigured with `speed 100` and `duplex full`. One of the most difficult features to get used to if you are familiar with Catalyst switches are the commands that substitute `vlan-switch` for the familiar and simple `vlan` in commands like:

show vlan-switch brief

The other annoying fact (if you have an older version of IOS) is that the switch still uses the `vlan database` style commands, although there are some macros that will get loaded and help you out if your IOS is new enough, such as an exec macro *vl* that will expand to `show vlan-switch brief`.

One thing you can do though is to practice creating **VLAN interfaces**, and therefore, layer 3 switching between VLANs. You can also configure EtherChannel, which is not quite the same as Port Channel, but relies on similar concepts.

Terminal tips

One of the first customizations users often make with GNS3 is the terminal application. The particular terminal application you use will depend on your underlying operating system and working out exactly what parameters you need to pass to your favorite application can be a mind-boggling experience. Luckily, there have been many enthusiasts who have contributed carefully crafted commands to launch a variety of terminal applications.

The terminal application is actually the part of GNS3 that you spend most time using, so making sure you have the right application, and settings that work best for you, is worth some effort. A summary of terminal application features that have pre-configured setting in GNS3 can be found at `http://rednectar.net/2013/09/09/a-comparison-of-gns3-terminal-applications/`. Choosing a good terminal application can save you a lot of configuration and debugging time. Some terminals have better support for some features than others. The features I find most useful are:

- **Tabbed and multi-windowed (tiled) interface**: I can have console sessions to ten or more routers going simultaneously. I don't want to have to cycle through ten or more windows to find the window I want. At times, I also like to have several windows tiled side by side, so a terminal application that supports both is ideal. SuperPutty, Secure CRT (Windows version only), and iTerm2 are examples.

- **Simultaneous input to multiple sessions**: I like to be able to type a command like `show ip route` once, and have it appear in all terminal sessions simultaneously. Some terminal applications (SuperPutty, SecureCRT) allow a line to be typed and then sent to all open windows. Better still, some applications (iTerm2, Konsole) allow even single characters to be sent to multiple windows, making it possible to use the *<Tab>* key for autocomplete.

- **Transparency**: Being able to see the GNS3 Workspace behind my terminal application can be very helpful, especially if I have labeled it well.

In this section, I will show you how to change the terminal application for your operating system, how Dynamips gives your terminal application access to the router console, and how to troubleshoot console connection issues.

Using a different terminal application

No matter which operating system you are using, changing the terminal application always starts at **General** settings of the GNS3 **Preferences** dialog under the **Terminal Settings** tab. To change your **Terminal** application for Router/ASA/Junos access, the GNS3 developers have provided a convent drop-down menu of **common** command-line launches for various Terminal applications.

The key to understanding how the **Preconfigured terminal commands** work is to realize that the drop-down menu simply gives you a selection of things that you could type in the **Terminal command:** field.

To actually choose one of them you have to both select the application you wish to use and click on **Use**. But even then, clicking on **Use** simply types the appropriate command in the **Terminal command:** field for you (wiping out whatever was there previously), ready for you to edit and personalize. You still have to hit **OK** when you have finished.

The drop-down list is different for each operating system, but the three-step action ((1) select, (2) click on **Use**, (3) click on **OK**) required to change console application is the same.

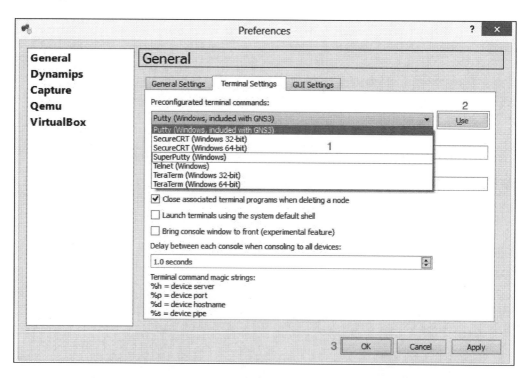

Once you have selected your console application, you will see that the command line will contain references to %**d**, %**h**, and %**p**. These variables refer to *device name*, *device server* (host IP), and *device port* (host port) respectively.

Using the AUX port

Occasionally, it is handy to have two separate console terminal sessions running at the same time. If you open a second normal console session, then the output of one session will be echoed in the other. However, if you open your second terminal session to the AUX port, it will be a different and independent session. One of the most useful applications for this is when you are debugging. You can have the output of a debug command displayed in the console session, while you issue commands in the other session, without the interference of the debug session.

To open a console terminal using the AUX port, select your device and navigate to **Device | Console via AUX port**.

Troubleshooting a device console

If you cannot gain access to a device's console, the very first thing you should check is which port number Dynamips has assigned to the console (issue a `show device` command in the **GNS3 Management Console** window to find out). See if your host has an open connection to that port by using the *netstat* command, substituting the console port number for *xxxx* in the following commands:

Windows	*netstat –na	find "xxxx"*
OSX/Linux	*netstat –na	grep xxxx*

If there are open connections or if the connections have not closed properly, then waiting a while may see them disappear or you may have to kill the process that has the ports opened. If you do not see open connections, you should be able to issue a *telnet 127.0.0.1 xxxx* where xxxx is the port number to see if you get a connection. If not, chances are that Dynamips has died.

Fine-tuning the topology – adding graphics and text

GNS3 graphical features are limited and the workspace was designed primarily for depicting images of devices and the links between them. However, there are some basic annotation tools on the **Annotate** menu. These are **Add Note**, **Insert picture**, **Draw rectangle**, and **Draw ellipse**. However, there are a couple of tricks that are worth knowing about that will give you a little less frustration at the limitation of these simple functions:

- **Rotation of shapes**: When you add a shape (not a picture) you can use the *<Alt>* + *p* and *<Alt>* + *m* or *<Alt>* + *<minus>* and *<Alt>* + *<plus>* keys to rotate a shape around its original top right-hand corner. In the case of a **Text** object, **you must have your cursor positioned in the text box** for this function to work.

  ○ Alternatively, you can right-click on the object and select **Style**, and enter a numeric value in the **Rotation:** field. This is often the easiest way to reset the shape to its original orientation.

- **Raising and lowering levels**: If you have overlapping shapes, especially if they are a solid color, then you often want to rearrange them to be in a different order. Right-clicking on a device and selecting **Raise one layer** or **Lower one layer** allows you to achieve this.

- **The background layer**: If you continue to lower the layer of an object, it eventually becomes a background object. The advantage of this is that once an object is in a background layer, it can't be accidently selected as you click on the workspace, you have to right-click on it and raise it again if you wish to manipulate it further. The background layer is also a fine place to put a standard background image such as a personalized identifier if you are sharing your designs.

In spite of the very limited graphic support, I have seen many examples where creative folk have made extremely attractive topologies.

Accessing GNS3 running on a remote machine

All the connections between routers, between your routers and your VPCS, and between your routers and your console are simply UDP or TCP connections on 127.0.0.1. If you know what port numbers are being used, it is a simple process to connect to that port from a different computer. There are two scenarios discussed

here: *Accessing a device console remotely* and *Linking GNS3 topologies on different hosts.*
A third method, the *Remote hypervisor* is discussed in *Chapter 7, Tips for Teachers,
Troubleshooters, and Team Leaders.*

Accessing a device console remotely

Before you can access the console remotely from another computer, you have to
understand how Dynamips gives you access to the console on your local computer.

Dynamips directs the console and AUX physical ports to logical TCP connections.
When you start a console session from GNS3, you are actually creating a telnet session
to Dynamips, not a serial console connection like on a real router. By default, GNS3
sets the first router to listen on port 2101 (earlier versions used 2000 or 2001 by
default) for the console connection and 2501 for the AUX port. So to set up a console
session to the Dynamips simulated router, all you have to do is telnet to your local
computer's relevant TCP port to access the virtual console or AUX router port. You of
course already know that the internal IP of your computer is 127.0.0.1, so in other
words you telnet to 127.0.0.1:2101 to get a console session with your first router.

This actually has some implications. For instance, you could access your console by
telnetting to port 2101 on your host computer's IP address from another computer.
But there is a catch. Since a bug fix in Dynamips, you have to change the host
binding for Dynamips from 127.0.0.1 to 0.0.0.0 to allow this.

This exercise is going to require the use of two networked computers. One of them
will be running GNS3, the other a console application like Windows Telnet Client or
OS X Terminal. Make sure you know the IP address of the GNS3 host computer.

On your GNS3 machine, check GNS3 **Preferences**, **Dynamips** settings under the
Hypervisor Manager tab to make sure that the **IP/Host binding** is set to 0.0.0.0.
Now create a topology with two routers. Connect them and start them, but do not
open the console. Hover your mouse over the router icons in turn and note the port
numbers being used for telnet and AUX connections. By default, these will be 2101
and 2501 respectively on the router you added first to your topology and 2102 and
2502 on the second.

On the computer not running GNS3, open a telnet session to the IP of the GNS3 host
using the port number for the console. If the GNS3 computer is at 192.168.1.1 and
your console on 2101, the command to run Telnet Client would be:

telnet 192.168.1.1 2101

And to telnet to the AUX port if it was at 2501:

telnet 192.168.1.1 2501

The result should be that you have access to the console of the GNS3 router running on the remote machine. But you can take this concept even further and have the GNS3 topology of one computer linked to the GNS3 topology of another.

Linking GNS3 topologies on different hosts

For this exercise your two networked computers need to be both running GNS3. Let's assume the two computers have IP addresses `192.168.1.1` and `192.168.1.2`.

On each computer, create a topology with a single router and cloud (or host) icon. On each computer, configure your cloud with an NIO_UDP port choose **Local port:** *5000*, **Remote host:** *192.168.1.x* and **Remote port:** *5000*, where *x* is the IP address of the other computer.

You can now link your router interfaces to the cloud NIO_UDP port you just created and configure your routers with IP addresses on the same subnet.

If you wished to create a second connection, you would of course have to use a port number other than `5000` on the second connection. Any free UDP port number can be used.

In *Chapter 6, Peeking under the GNS3 Hood*, more details of how you can use TCP and UDP connections between multiple devices is given.

Summary

This chapter has explored some of the more advanced features of GNS3 including the important and sometimes difficult tasks of connecting to the outside world.

You have seen how to choose an alternate console application and potentially modify the way it behaves, and to use it more effectively to access remote consoles as well.

By now you have a simulation environment ready to build as sophisticated a Cisco router network as your hardware allows. It's time to look at other simulated hardware. In the next chapter, you will discover how to simulate Cisco Adaptive Security Appliances (ASAs), Juniper routers, Vyatta routers, Linux and even Windows simulated computers.

4
Unleashing Other Emulators

GNS3 is most famous for emulating Cisco routers using the Dynamips emulator. But GNS3 also comes with other emulators, Qemu, Pemu and VirtualBox, and between them Cisco ASAs, PIX firewalls, Juniper routers, Linux, and Windows PCs can be emulated. This chapter show takes you step-by-step through some of the possibilities.

The following topics will be covered in this chapter:

- The Qemu emulator:
    - Adding Qemu support
    - Microcore Linux using Qemu
    - Adding ASA firewalls
    - Adding Juniper routers (Junos)

- The VirtualBox emulator:
    - Adding VirtualBox support
    - A Linux PC on VirtualBox
    - A Windows PC on VirtualBox
    - Vyatta router on VirtualBox

By the end of this chapter, you will have a variety of simulation options, ready to tackle some extremely diverse simulations.

The Qemu emulator

Like *Dynamips*, *Qemu* is an emulator. In fact, it gets its name by claiming to be a **Q**uick **EMU**lator. And it is actually able to emulate many more devices than Dynamips, such as Linux servers and Windows PCs, but in the GNS3 environment it is most often used to emulate other networking devices such as Cisco ASAs and Juniper routers.

Adding Qemu support

Also like Dynamips, you will need more than just Qemu. You will also need a binary copy of the operating system you want Qemu to emulate. And because you want to use GNS3 to configure connections between your Qemu devices and even your Dynamips devices, you will also need a third piece of code called `qemuwrapper`, which is included with your GNS3 install.

And one more thing. The version of Qemu you run has to be aware of the types of interfaces used in GNS3. GNS3 creates UDP tunnels between devices to allow them to communicate (see *Chapter 6, Peeking under the GNS3 hood*), so you need a specially patched version of Qemu that knows how to interpret the `-net type udp` parameter that will be passed to the emulator on startup.

 Versions of Qemu later than 1.1 support UDP tunnel interfaces, but to make them support the Cisco ASA you have to adjust other parameters.

Windows and OS X users would have installed a copy of Qemu binary that is already patched when they installed GNS3, and can now continue at the *Qemu preferences* section dicussed later in this chapter. Linux users need to download the patched version first.

Linux

Here is how to download and install Qemu 0.11.0. I chose this version because it is already patched and it is proven to work.

wget http://sourceforge.net/projects/
gns-3/files/Qemu/Linux/QEMU-0.11.0-GNS3-Ubuntu-Linux.tgz

tar xvf QEMU-0.11.0-GNS3-Ubuntu-Linux.tgz

cd QEMU-0.11.0-GNS3-Ubuntu-Linux

sudo ./Qinstall

When you configure Qemu in the next section, use these values:

`Path to Qemuwrapper:` */usr/share/gns3/qemuwrapper.py*

`Path to qemu:` *qemu*

`Path to qemu-img:` *qemu-img*

Qemu preferences

Start by navigating to GNS3 **Preferences** | the **Qemu** settings | the **General Settings** tab.

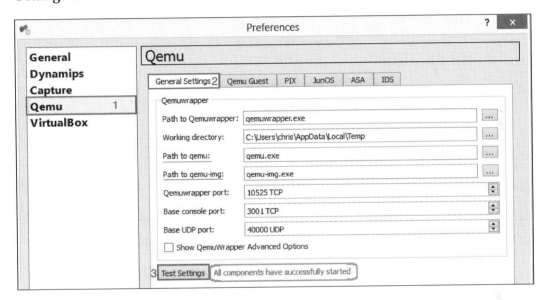

Click on the **Test Settings** button to ensure that your OS has paths to **qemuwrapper**, **qemu** and **qemu-img**. If not, check your GNS3 install directory and make sure these files are present. If necessary, specify the exact path to each by clicking on the ellipsis (**...**) next to the field where these paths are defined and find the appropriate directories. Windows users should use the preceding illustration as a guide, Linux users refer to the previous section, and OS X users should use the following:

`Path to Qemuwrapper:` */Applications/GNS3.app/Contents/Resources/qemuwrapper.py*

`Path to qemu:` */Applications/GNS3.app/Contents/Resources/Qemu-0.11.0/bin/qemu*

`Path to qemu-img:` */Applications/GNS3.app/Contents/Resources/Qemu-0.11.0/bin/qemu-img*

If your settings are correct, you are ready to emulate your chosen OS using Qemu. I suggest that you start with a Linux guest, such as Microcore Linux.

Microcore Linux using Qemu

Probably, the easiest operating system to get Qemu to emulate is Microcore Linux. It is worth getting comfortable setting up Linux before tackling more specialized operating systems, like Cisco ASA or Juniper Junos.

 Note: You must have set up Qemu as described in the preceding *Adding Qemu support* section.

Step 1: Download a Qemu guest

Download and save a copy of Microcore Linux from `http://www.gns3.net/appliances/`. Create a `Qemu` directory off your `Images` directory and save your copy of your chosen image there.

Step 2: Configure Qemu preferences

Back at the GNS3 **Preferences**, the **Qemu** settings (1) at the **Qemu Guest** tab (2), choose an **Identifier name** (I chose *LinuxMicrocore*) (3) then click on the ellipsis (...) next to the **Binary image** field (4) and select the copy of Micorcore Linux you downloaded in Step 1.

 Make sure you click on **Save** (5), and can see your saved image in the list of **Qemu Guest Images** at the bottom of the dialogue (6) before you click on **OK**.

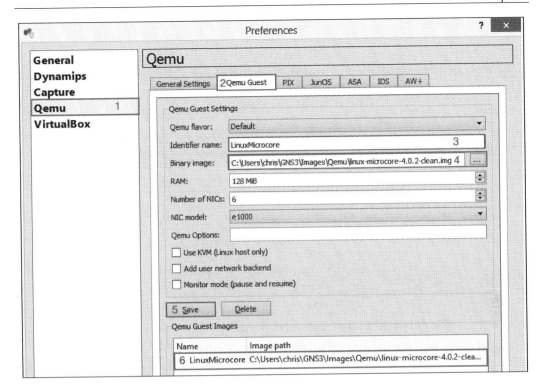

Step 3: Create a topology using your Qemu box

Start and name a new project in GNS3. GNS3 will automatically save your Qemu virtual hard drive in a file called FLASH that will be stored in a directory named after the hostname (for example, LinuxMicrocore) in a **qemu-flash-files** directory off your Project_Name directory, so there is no need to check any options on the **New Project** dialogue.

Add a Cisco router of your favorite kind. Then click on the **End devices** icon in **Devices toolbar**, and you will see that **Qemu guest** is now an available option. Click on **Qemu guest** and drag it into your topology.

Use the **Add a link** tool to connect the **LinuxMicrocore** host **e0** interface to the **R1 f0/0** interface.

Next, click on **Control | Start/Resume all devices** to start your router and your Qemu host. There should be a console window open to give you a command line access to your Qemu LinuxMicrocore host.

Step 4: Configure IP addresses

To prove connectivity, assign an IP address to **eth0** on QEMU1 host by issuing the following command in the **LinuxMicrocore** host console window:

`tc@box:~$` *sudo ifconfig eth0 10.1.1.2 netmask 255.255.255.0*

> Press *<Ctrl>+<Alt>* to allow your cursor to exit the **LinuxMicrocore** host window.

And assign an IP address to the **f0/0** interface of the router like this:

R1#configure terminal

`R1(config)#`*interface f0/0*

`R1(config-if)#`*ip address 10.1.1.1 255.255.255.0*

`R1(config-if)#`*no shutdown*

`R1(config-if)#`*end*

Then test connectivity with a ping:

R1#ping 10.1.1.2

```
Type escape sequence to abort.
Sending 5, 100-byte ICMP Echos to 10.1.1.2, timeout is 2 seconds:
.!!!!
Success rate is 80 percent (4/5), round-trip min/avg/max = 8/18/20 ms
```

Some people prefer using Qemu Linux hosts to using VPCs to test connectivity between devices. A Qemu Linux host like this can have the advantage of being able to be configured as an FTP server, DNS server, or even a DHCP server if you require such a server in your network, but to deploy many of them requires many more host resources than the simple VPCs.

Step 5: Save your configuration in Microcore Linux

Microcore Linux will lose any configuration changes you make when you power down the virtual machine. There is however an editable script (`/opt/bootlocal.sh`) that is executed each time the virtual machine starts, and a there is a process to save this script.

The only editor that comes installed with Microcore Linux is **vi**; you will have to start your edit session with the command:

sudo vi /opt/bootlocal.sh

```
Backing up files to /mnt/sda1/tce/mydata.tgz Done.
```

If you wish to keep your set IP address for **eth0** to be **10.1.1.2/24**, your default gateway to be **10.1.1.1** and your hostname to be **qemu1**, add the following lines to this file:

sudo ifconfig eth0 10.1.1.2 netmask 255.255.255.0

sudo route add default gw 10.1.1.1

sudo hostname qemu1

And if you are not familiar with how to use **vi**, then read the information available at: `http://www.unix-manuals.com/tutorials/vi/vi-in-10-1.html`. In short, you will have to press *i* (for insert), move the cursor to the end, add the lines, then press the five-key sequence *<Esc>:wq<Enter>*.

Once you have saved your changes in **vi**, you will also have to save this configuration using the `filetool.sh` script like the following:

filetool.sh -b

A couple of other useful Microcore Linux commands you might need to use are:

sudo reboot

sudo poweroff

> Users who want to do anything more with Microcore Linux should read `wiki.tinycorelinux.net/wiki:persistence_for_dummies`.
>
> If you find that your IP address has disappeared after rebooting, try running the `bootlocal.sh` script from the command line:
>
> */opt/bootlocal.sh*

Now that you have a simple image operating in the Qemu emulator, you might like to try something more adventurous, like a Cisco ASA firewall.

Adding ASA firewalls

The process of running an ASA is similar to running Microcore Linux, but has an added complication that the **Linux kernel** (vmlinuz) and **initial ramdisk** (initrd) have to be extracted from the ASA binary image and loaded separately into Qemu, so there is a special page in your settings to allow for this.

> You must have set up Qemu as described in the preceding *Adding Qemu support* section, before adding ASA firewalls.

Step 1: Unpack your ASA binary

I will assume that you have a copy of an ASA 8.4(2) binary (`asa842-k8.bin`) that you have copied from your installation CD, or downloaded from `Cisco.com`. The unpacking procedure detailed here only works with this version, and has been adapted from the procedures detailed on the Dynamips forum at `http://7200emu.hacki.at/viewtopic.php?t=9074` and only works on Linux. Once these files have been created, they can be copied and used on Windows or OS X.

> Remember, the following process only works for **Linux**. It will create the files `asa842-initrd.gz` and `asa842-vmlinuz` that you will need in the next step.

Create a new directory called `ASA` in your `Images` directory then copy your binary file `asa842-k8.bin` to this directory. Also place in this directory a copy of the shell utility `repack.v4.sh.gz` which you can download (after you have logged in, create an account if necessary) from `http://7200emu.hacki.at/viewtopic.php?t=9074` (search for the word **download** within this post to find the link.)

Next, open a terminal window and change directory to your newly created `ASA` directory, and unpack the shell script, then run the script as root. You should see three files created. Use the following output as a guide (Note, after some initial output, the script takes some time to complete):

```
cd ~/GNS3/Images/ASA
gunzip repack.v4.sh.gz
chmod +x repack.v4.sh
sudo ./repack.v4.sh
Repack script version: 4
no syslinux/cdrtools - ISO creation skipped
<...output omitted...>
ls
asa842-initrd.gz            asa842-vmlinuz
asa842-initrd-original.gz  asa842-k8.bin            repack.v4.sh
```

Note in particular the files `asa842-initrd.gz` and `asa842-vmlinuz`. You will need these in the next step. If you want to use these files on Windows, copy these files to a your Windows computer's `Images\ASA` (or Macintosh's `Images/ASA`) directory, creating the directory if necessary.

Step 2: Configure Qemu/ASA Preferences

Open GNS3 **Preferences**, **Qemu** settings (1), **ASA** tab (2).

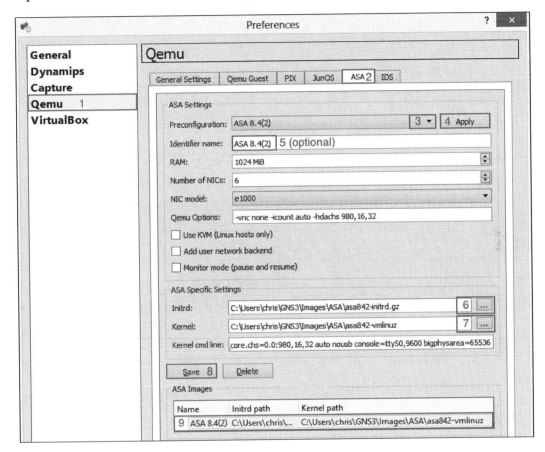

You will see that there is a **Preconfiguration** setting with an option to preconfigure this page with the settings for a number of popular ASA image versions. This exercise is using ASA version 8.4(2), so select **ASA 8.4(2)** from the drop-down list (3) then click on the **Apply** button (4) to pre-populate the page with the correct settings for this image. In the **ASA Specific Settings** section, click on the ellipsis (**...**) for both the **Initrd:** (6) and the **Kernel:** fields (7) and choose respectively the `asa842-initrd.gz` and the `asa842-vmlinuz` files you created in the previous step.

Make sure you click on **Save** (8), and can see your saved image in the list of **ASA Images** at the bottom of the dialogue (9) before you click on **OK**.

Step 3: Create a topology using your ASA

Start and name a new project in GNS3. GNS3 will automatically save your ASA virtual hard drive in a file called FLASH that will be stored in a directory named after the hostname (for example, ASA1) in a **qemu-flash-files** directory off your Project_ Name directory, so there is no need to check any options on the **New Project** dialogue.

When you select the **Security Device** icon in the **Devices Toolbar**, you will now see that **ASA Firewall** is no longer greyed out and can be selected. Add a router and an ASA to your topology and connect interface **f0/0** on the router to **e0** on the ASA.

Step 4: Configure IP addresses

Start your devices by clicking on **Control | Start/Resume all devices**.

> ASAs do not have a virtual screen like you see when you use Qemu to emulate a Linux machine. You will have to access the ASA using the console connection, just like in the real world. You may still see a window open showing the BIOS boot up, but you cannot access the ASA from this screen.

Access the consoles of your router and ASA by clicking on **Control | Console connect to all devices**. It may take some time for the devices to boot up.

> When Qemu emulates an ASA, it has the same problem as Dynamips, and is likely to run your CPU at 100%. However, there is no Idle-PC setting for Qemu or ASAs. There are, however, ways to limit the CPU usage for any particular application. Two of these (**BES** and **cpulimit**) are discussed on the GNS3 website available at:http://www.gns3. net/documentation/gns3/pix-firewall-emulation/. If you have trouble starting multiple devices, you may have more success if you start them one at a time.

You should now be able to configure IP addresses so that these devices can at least ping each other.

And assign an IP address to the **f0/0** interface of the router like this:

R1#configure terminal

R1(config) #*interface f0/0*

R1(config-if) #*ip address 10.1.1.2 255.255.255.0*

R1(config-if) #*no shutdown*

R1(config-if) #*end*

If you are unfamiliar with the Cisco ASA syntax, use the following example as a guide:

```
ciscoasa> enable
Password: <Enter>
ciscoasa# configure terminal
ciscoasa(config)# interface gigabitEthernet 0
ciscoasa(config-if)# nameif outside
INFO: Security level for "outside" set to 0 by default.
ciscoasa(config-if)# ip address 10.1.1.1 255.255.255.0
ciscoasa(config-if)# no shutdown
```

Now check your ip config, and test with a ping:

```
ciscoasa(config-if)# show interface ip brief | exclude down
Interface          IP-Address     OK? Method   Status          Protocol
GigabitEthernet0   10.1.1.1       YES manual   up              up
ciscoasa(config-if)# ping 10.1.1.2
Type escape sequence to abort.
Sending 5, 100-byte ICMP Echos to 10.1.1.2, timeout is 2 seconds:
.!!!!
Success rate is 80 percent (4/5), round-trip min/avg/max = 9/12/17 ms
```

Step 5: Save your ASA config

As with working with routers, you must always save your configuration from within the simulated environment, so with your ASA, make sure you issue the *copy running-config startup-config* command, or more simply, the *write memory* command:

```
ciscoasa# write memory
```

GNS3 does NOT extract the configuration from ASA devices and save it in the `configs` directory, instead it will always create a `qemu-flash-drives` directory and your ASA virtual hard drives (containing your configurations) will be saved in a directory named after your device in this directory.

Finally, to save your router config and your topology file, navigate to **File | Save Project**.

Adding Juniper routers (Junos)

The process of running Junos is similar to running Microcore Linux, except that Junos runs on BSD Unix so what you will actually be doing is setting up a BSD virtual machine that is dedicated to running a single application, the Juniper Operating System (Junos). When Junos is operating in this mode (rather than on Juniper hardware) it is usually referred to as "**Olive**".

 You must have set up Qemu as described in the preceding *Adding Qemu support* section.

Step 1: Prepare the required files

You will need two source files and a patching script before you commence. Create a new directory called `Junos` in your `Images` directory and place the following files there.

1. The `freebsd-4.11.img` file from the `http://www.gns3.net/appliances` page. This is a patched version of **FreeBSD 4.11 ready for Junos**.

2. Your copy of the Junos operating system. It will be a file with a name something like `jinstall-9.6R1.13-domestic-signed.tgz`.

3. The `junos-auto-fix-checkpic` script files from `http://forum.gns3.net/download/file.php?id=2018` (Windows) or `http://forum.gns3.net/download/file.php?id=2019` (Linux/OS X). Place the unzipped file(s) in your `Junos` directory. Linux/OS X users will have just a script file: `junos-auto-fix-checkpic.sh`. Windows users will have a batch file: `junos-auto-fix-checkpic.bat` and a `bin` directory.

Copy your base image to a name that will reflect the version of Junos you plan to install. In this example, I will use `jinstall-9.6R1.13-domestic-signed.tgz`, so I use the name `olive-9.6R1.13.img`. The copy will be the base file for the future operations.

Linux and OS X

cd ~\Images\Junos

cp freebsd-4.11.img olive-9.6R1.13.img

Windows

cd "\%HOMEPATH%\Images\Junos"

copy freebsd-4.11.img olive-9.6R1.13.img

Step 2: Patch Junos source image

The Junos image as it is when downloaded from the Juniper website contains a section of code known as `checkpic` which lives in an archive called `pkgtools.tgz` within the image, in several places. To make your copy of Junos run on something that is not Juniper hardware, these sections of code have to be patched. This is done using the script you have just downloaded from the GNS3 website.

Run the script from a command prompt from your `Junos` directory. If your Junos image is called `jinstall-9.6R1.13-domestic-signed.tgz`, then the command you will use will be as follows:

- **For Linux and OS X**

  sudo ./junos-auto-fix-checkpic.sh jinstall-9.6R1.13-domestic-signed.tgz

- **For Windows**

  junos-auto-fix-checkpic.bat jinstall-9.6R1.13-domestic-signed.tgz

The script will parse the source file and find all instances of the `pkgtools.tgz` archive file (there are several instances), unpack them, locate the script file called `checkpic` inside the archive, modify the `checkpic` script (to simply say `exit 0`) then repack the archive and recalculate the md5 checksums where necessary then write the output to a new image called `jinstall-9.6R1.13-domestic-olive.tgz`. The script then creates an ISO image from this file. It is this ISO image that you will need in the next step.

Step 3: Install Junos

All that is left to do now is to physically get the patched Olive image into the Free BSD image and installed.

Task 1: Launch Qemu

Start by launching your FreeBSD virtual machine with 1G RAM, otherwise the install might fail.

Linux

qemu -m 1G -hda olive-9.6R1.13.img -cdrom jinstall-9.6R1.13-domestic-olive.iso

OS X

/Applications/GNS3.app/Contents/Resources/Qemu-0.11.0/bin/qemu –m 1G -hda olive-9.6R1.13.img -cdrom jinstall-9.6R1.13-domestic-olive.iso

Windows

"%PROGRAMFILES%\GNS3\qemu.exe" -m 1G -hda olive-9.6R1.13.img -cdrom jinstall-9.6R1.13-domestic-olive.iso

Task 2: Install Junos files

1. When the image boots, login with the username of *root*. The password is also *root*.

2. Install the Junos software using the following commands:

    mount /cdrom

    `#Note: press <Enter> one more time once the mount is done`

    pkg_add -f /cdrom/jinstall-9.6R1.13-domestic-olive.tgz

     Be patient. Very patient. There will be no visible output, but you can keep checking that `olive-9.6R1.13.img` is growing. Eventually you should see that the screen displays a message saying that:
    A REBOOT IS REQUIRED TO LOAD THIS SOFTWARE CORRECTLY

3. However, you need to do this reboot carefully, because from this point onwards your Virtual Machine is going to behave like a Juniper router, which sends most of its output to the serial console port, so you will have to do something about that.

4. Start by shutting down FreeBSD using the *halt* command:

    # halt

5. When you see the message saying that **The operating system has halted**, quit Qemu by pressing *<Ctrl>+<Alt>+2* and entering the *quit* command.

    (qemu) *quit*

     In Qemu, you can return to the guest OS by pressing *<Ctrl>+<Alt>+1*.

Task 3: Boot your image with console access

From this point you will want serial console access to your Junos router, so you need to boot your image much the same way as it will be booted in GNS3 and access the console via a telnet session just like your Cisco routers.

1. Use this command to boot your router with console access via TCP port `3001`. The `server` option in the command line tells Qemu to wait for a telnet session to be established before booting:

   Linux

   *qemu -m 1G -hda olive-9.6R1.13.img *
   -serial telnet:0.0.0.0:3001,server

   OS X

   */Applications/GNS3.app/Contents/Resources/Qemu-0.11.0/bin/qemu *
   *–m 1G -hda olive-9.6R1.13.img *
   –serial telnet:0.0.0.0:3001,server

   Windows

   "%PROGRAMFILEs%\GNS3\qemu.exe" -m 1G -hda olive-9.6R1.13.img -serial
   telnet:0.0.0.0:3001,server

2. This command will only initiate the boot. For the boot process to continue, you must start a telnet session to `127.0.0.1` on port `3001`. For example:

   telnet 127.0.0.1 3001

   The output from the boot process will continue in your telnet session, and the install process will complete, and again, **extreme** patience is required (5-20 min). If you insist on watching, you will see your router reboot about half way through the process, and finally you will get to the login prompt. Note that your Qemu session will also open, but not all of the output will be seen there. If you monitor your `olive-9.6R1.13.img` file, you will see it grow in size during this process.

3. In the QEMU window, login with the username *root* and no password.

4. Shutdown the router with the *halt* command:

   `root@% halt`

5. Once your router has shutdown (watch your telnet session for the messages), exit Qemu in the usual way (*<Ctrl>+<Alt>+2*, then *quit*). Your Junos image is now ready for use in GNS3.

Step 4: Configure Qemu/JunOS Preferences

In GNS3, open GNS3 **Preferences**, **Qemu** (1) settings at the **JunOS** tab (2).

Give your image a name in the **Identifier name:** field, such as *JunOS9.6R1.13* (4).

In the **Binary image:** field, click on the ellipsis (**...**) and locate the `olive-9.6R1.13.img` file in your `Junos` directory (3).

Check that the **RAM:** value is *512 MiB* (5).

Check that the **NIC model:** is **E1000** (6).

> Make sure you click **Save** (7), and can see your saved image in the list of **JunOS Images** at the bottom of the dialog (8) before you click on **OK**.

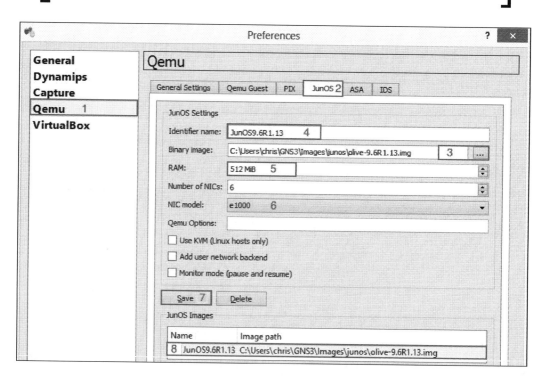

Step 5: Create a topology using your Junos router

Start and name a new project in GNS3. GNS3 will automatically save your JUNOS virtual hard drive in a file called `FLASH` that will be stored in a directory named after the hostname (for example, `JUNOS1`) in a **qemu-flash-files** directory off your `Project_Name` directory, so there is no need to check any options on the **New Project** dialogue.

When you select the **Router Device** icon in the **Devices Toolbar**, you will now see that **Juniper router** is no longer greyed out and can be selected. Add two Juniper routers to your topology and connect interface **e0** on one router to **e0** on the other.

Step 6: Configure IP addresses

Start your devices by navigating to **Control | Start/Resume all devices**.

You will see the Juniper routers inside the Qemu screen, but the output will be directed to the console. You will have to access the Juniper router using the console connection, just like in the real world.

Access the consoles of your routers by navigating to **Control | Console connect to all devices**. It may take some minutes for the devices to boot up. Eventually you will see the **login:** prompt. Login with the username *root* and no password is required.

You may find that your cursor moves up several lines after logging in. Look for your cursor, not for output on the command line.

Before you can make any changes to the configuration, you will have to create a password with characters that include a change of case, digits or punctuation, like the following:

root@% *cli*

root> *edit*

`Entering configuration mode`

`[edit]`

root# set system root-authentication plain-text-password

New password: *Password*

Retype new password: *Password*

The Qemu **e0** interface is called the **em0** interface on the Juniper, so to configure an IP address for the first interface you can follow the following example:

root# *set interfaces em0 unit 0 family inet address 10.1.1.1/24*

`[edit]`

root# *commit*

`commit complete`

Repeat the preceding configuration for the other router using an IP address of `10.1.1.2/24` and the routers should be able to ping each other:

```
root# exit
Exiting configuration mode
root> ping 10.1.1.1
PING 10.1.1.2 (10.1.1.1): 56 data bytes
64 bytes from 10.1.1.1: icmp_seq=0 ttl=64 time=5391.740 ms
^c
```

Step 7: Save your Juniper config

Unlike when working with Dynamips, GNS3 does *not* extract the configuration from Juniper routers and save it in the `configs` directory. Instead, it will always create a `qemu-flash-drives` directory and your Juniper routers' virtual hard drives (containing your configurations) are saved in a directory named after your device.

Juniper routers save their configuration to flash every time you use the **commit** command. But you will still have to save your topology file that contains the information about which devices are connected to which. To save your topology file, navigate to **File** | **Save Project**.

The VirtualBox emulator

VirtualBox is another emulator like Qemu. In fact, there is a bit if a love/hate relationship between the supporters of Qemu versus the supporters of VirtualBox. Qemu is more lightweight, while VirtualBox is more feature rich! In any case, let me describe how to set up VirtualBox on your system, and then you can decide.

The VirtualBox application does not come with the GNS3 install. Before you can begin to think about running VirtualBox (VB) emulations, you will have to download and install the VB package from `https://www.virtualbox.org/wiki/Downloads`. Linux users will also need to also install **xdotool**.

Adding VirtualBox support

Assuming you have **VirtualBox (VB)** installed on your system, you now have to configure GNS3 with the details of your VB installation.

Start by opening the GNS3 **Preferences**, **VirtualBox** settings, **General Settings** tab.

The default settings should be all you need, but make sure you click on the **Test Settings** button to be sure. If you see a message saying **VirtualBox is not installed**, then you need to check your VirtualBox installation. If you see a message saying **Failed to start xdotool** then you need to install xdotool (*sudo apt-get install xdotool*).

Unlike Dynamips or Qemu, VirtualBox needs to be setup with its set of virtual machines *outside* of GNS3.

A Windows PC on Oracle VirtualBox

I will assume you already have a CD or ISO file for Windows XP. If not, the process will be more or less the same for any other version of Windows, but XP has a light footprint so is probably the most suitable for the GNS3 environment.

Step 1: Create a Windows XP virtual machine

Start your Oracle VirtualBox application and create a new virtual machine (**Machine | New**). Give it a name that reflects the image you are about to create, such as *WinXP*, check the **Type** and **Version** are correct and click on **Next**.

Accept the default values for **Memory size** and **Hard drive**, but I suggest that you choose **VMDK** as the **Hard drive file type** in case you ever want to use this machine with VMware.

Let the **Storage on physical hard drive** be **Dynamically allocated**, and accept the default **File location and size** to complete the creation of your virtual machine.

There are still a few settings that have to be set before you can create for Virtual Machine. Navigate to **Machine | Settings** and choose the **Storage** option (1, in the following figure). In the **Storage Tree** area, you will see that the DVD/CD icon shows **Empty**.

Click on this **Empty** entry (2), then click on the DVD/CD icon in the **Attributes** area (3) and select the drive (or **Virtual CD/DVD disk file...**) where you have your original copy of your Window XP CD (4), before finally clicking on **OK** (5).

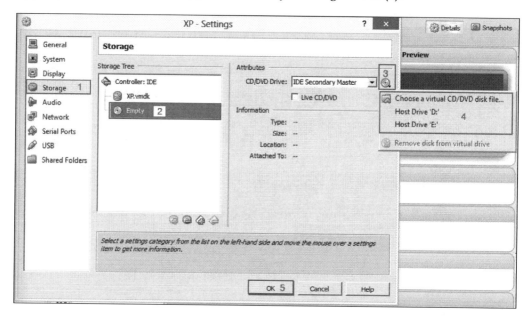

Now start your virtual machine (**Machine | Start**). It will boot from your Window XP CD (or ISO) where you can complete your installation and any updates you would like to install.

When you have completed the installation, shut down your Windows Virtual Machine. If you installed your VM from an ISO image, you will probably want to return to the **Machine | Settings** and change the **Storage** option so that you disassociate your ISO image.

Before you integrate your VM with GNS3, you will need to adjust the **Network** adapter settings. Start by choosing **File | Preferences**, and select the **Network** settings. You need to have at least one **VirtualBox Host-Only Ethernet Adapter** installed. If you do not have one, click on the **Add host-only network** icon to add one. Next, select your WinXP machine, and navigate to **Machine | Settings** and select the **Network** option. Click on the tab for **Adapter 2**, and check the **Enable Network Adapter** option. In the **Attached to:** drop-down, select **Host-only Adapter**, and click on **OK**. You can now shut down the Oracle VirtualBox Manger application.

Step 2: Configure GNS3 for your VM

Start GNS3 and open GNS3 **Preferences, VirtualBox** settings (1), **VirtualBox Guest** tab (2), and you will see that there is a drop-down selection for the **VM List:** (4) where you can choose any of the VirtualBox VMs that you have created. The first time you click on this drop-down, it is likely to be empty, so click on the **Refresh VM List** button (3) if this is the case.

Select your newly created VM from the list, and fill in the **Identifier name:** field (5) (I called mine *WinXP*) then click on **Save** (6), then click on **OK**.

 Make sure you click on **Save** (6), and can see your saved image in the list of **VirtualBox Machines** at the bottom of the dialogue (7) before you click on **OK**.

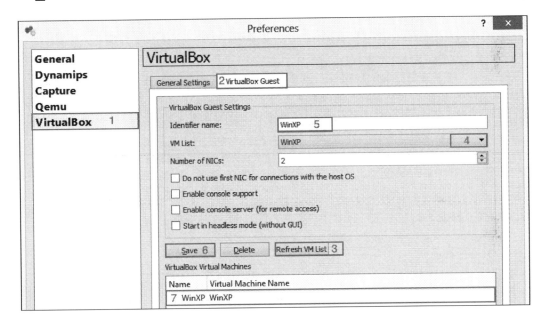

Click on the **End Device** icon from your **Devices** toolbar, and you will see that the **VirtualBox Guest** icon is no longer greyed out.

Step 3: Create a topology with a VirtualBox host

Add a VirtualBox guest and a router to the topology, and then link interface **e1** of the VB guest to interface **f0/0** of your router.

When you go to connect a link to the VB Guest, interface **e0** is greyed out. It is reserved as a kind of out-of-band management interface so your VM can still access the internet to receive updates via the host computer. If you wish, you can remove this feature by **unchecking** the **Reserve first NIC for VirtualBox NAT to host OS** option in your **VirtualBox Guest** settings, or temporarily disable it by disabling the interface either in the guest OS or in the **VM VirtualBox Manager**.

VirtualBox works quite differently to Qemu. There are two major differences:

1. Each virtual machine is an independent VM maintained by VirtualBox, not by GNS3. All configurations of your VMs will be kept inside each VM's Virtual HDD rather than in a FLASH file stored with your project.

2. You will have to create a new VM for every VM you wish to deploy in GNS3. To see this, just try and add another copy of your WinXP VM to your topology: you won't be able to. You will have to clone this VM, creating a new VM before you can add another.

Your WinXP host will be expecting to get an IP address via DHCP, so instead of starting all devices in your topology, click on just your router, and navigate to **Device | Start**, then navigate to **Device | Console**.

Configure your router with an IP address, and set it up as a DHCP server. Here is my configuration:

R1#configure terminal

R1(config)#*interface f0/0*

R1(config-if)#*ip address 10.1.1.1 255.255.255.0*

R1(config-if)#*no shutdown*

R1(config-if)#*exit*

R1(config)#*ip dhcp pool 10.1.1.0/24*

R1(dhcp-config)#*network 10.1.1.0 /24*

R1(dhcp-config)#*default-router 10.1.1.1*

R1(dhcp-config)#*end*

Now start your VirtualBox WinXP guest PC in GNS3. The VirtualBox application will start, and your guest PC will boot.

Your guest may start in the background, and even pop up a dialog that has to be answered. You may have to bring the VirtualBox application to the front before the startup process times out.

When your XP guest has finished booting, log in and you should see that it has obtained an IP address from your Cisco router assigned to **Ethernet Local Area Connection 2**. Verify your IP configuration by pinging the router from your guest VM.

A Linux PC on VirtualBox

Another way to add a VirtualBox host is to download a prepared image. There is a selection available at `http://www.gns3.net/appliances/` as well as many other places on the internet, but for this exercise I will use the same version of Linux that was used for the Qemu example, Microcore Linux, so download the *VirtualBox* image. VirtualBox stores images by default in a directory called `VirtualBox VMs` off your home folder (`~/VirtualBox VMs` or `%HOMEPATH%\VirtualBox VMs`), so save the downloaded file (`Linux Microcore 3.8.2.ova`) there.

Open the VirtualBox Manager and click on **File | Import Appliance**. In the **Import Virtual Appliance** dialogue, click on **Open appliance...** then and locate select the `Linux Microcore 3.8.2.ova` file. Click on **Next**, then click on **Import**.

Just as with the Windows VM, you will have to adjust the **Network** adapter settings, so click **Machine | Settings** and select the **Network** option. Click on the tab for **Adapter 2**, and check the **Enable Network Adapter** option. In the **Attached to:** drop-down, select **Host-only Adapter**, and click on **OK**.

From this point on, repeat **Step 2** and **Step 3** from the preceding *A Windows PC on Oracle VirtualBox* section.

Adding a Vyatta router using VirtualBox

For the final variation I will use a prepared `.vdi` (VirtualBox disk image) as the basis to create a VirtualBox VM. From `http://www.gns3.net/appliances/` download the Vyatta VirtualBox 6.5 appliance (if it is in `.rar` format, unpack it first) and store the `vyatta6.5vc.vdi` file in your `VirtualBox VMs` directory.

Step 1: Create a Vyatta virtual machine

Using the **VM VirtualBox Manager** application, choose **Machine | New**, then name your machine *Vyatta*, give it a **Type:** of *Linux*, **Version:** *Debian*, click on **Next**. Give the VM *512MB RAM*, click on **Next**. Choose **Do not add a virtual hard drive**, then click on **Create**, then **Continue**.

This action sets up the directory structure on your host computer for your new VM, but with no hard disk drive. You now need to copy the `vyatta6.5vc.vdi` file you downloaded to this directory.

Linux and OS X

cp ~/VirtualBox\ VMs/vyatta6.5vc.vdi ~/VirtualBox\ VMs/Vyatta

Windows

copy "%HOMEPATH%\VirtualBox VMs\vyatta6.5vc.vdi" "%HOMEPATH%\VirtualBox VMs\Vyatta"

Click **Machine | Settings**, and select the **System** settings. In the **Boot Order:** selection list, **uncheck** the **Floppy** option, and **uncheck** the **CD/DVD ROM** option. In the **Extended Features:** section, **uncheck** the **Enable absolute pointing device**.

Still in the **System** settings click on the **Processor** tab and set the **Execution Cap:** to *50%*.

Select the **Display** settings and reduce the **Video memory:** to *1 MB*. Ignore the warning that you have less than the required amount of video memory.

Select the **Storage** settings (1) and click on the **Controller:SATA** device in the **Storage Tree** area (2), then click on the blue **Add attachment** icon under the **Storage Tree** area (3), select **Add Hard Disk** (4) and select **Choose existing disk**. Finally, navigate to and choose the copy of the `vyatta6.5vc.vdi` file you copied to your `Vyatta` directory and click on **Open**.

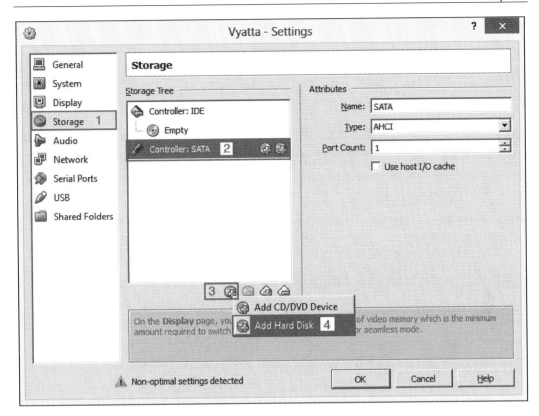

Select the **Audio** settings and **uncheck** the **Enable** audio option.

Select the **Network** settings and under the **Adapter 1** tab, the **Enable Network Adapter** should already be **checked**. Select the **Adapter 2** tab and **check** the **Enable Network Adapter**, and repeat for the **Adapter 3** and **Adapter 4** tabs. Don't worry that the adapters may not be **Attached to:** any device, GNS3 will take care of that later.

Select the **Serial Ports** settings and **check** the **Enable Serial Port** option.

Select the **USB** settings and **uncheck** the **Enable USB controller** option.

Click on **OK**.

Step 2: Clone your Vyatta router

You now have a clean unconfigured Vyatta router, but you are likely to want more than one. I suggest that you keep this initial router as a template and create two new clones ready for your lab.

In the **VM VirtualBox Manger**, select your newly created **Vyatta** VM, and then navigate to **Machine | Clone**. Name the clone *Vyatta1*, **check** the **Reinitialize the MAC address of all network cards**, click on **Next**, make the **Clone Type** a **Full Clone**, and click on **Clone**.

Repeat the process and create a clone called *Vyatta2*.

Step 3: Configure GNS3 for your VMs

Start GNS3 and open GNS3 **Preferences**, **VirtualBox** settings, **VirtualBox Guest** tab, and you will see that there is a drop-down selection for the **VM List**, Click on the **Refresh VM List** button if you don't see your newly created VMs.

Select the **Vyatta1** VM from the list, and fill in the **Identifier name:** field (I called mine *Vyatta1*), change the **Number of NICs** to *4*, **uncheck** the **Reserve first NIC for VirtualBox NAT to host OS**, then click on **Save**.

Repeat the process to add the **Vyatta2** VM to GNS3, and then click on **OK**.

Step 4: Create a topology with a Vyatta host

In GNS3, create a new topology and add the Vyatta VirtualBox guests (**Vyatta1** and **Vyatta2**) and a Cisco router to the topology.

If you don't like the default VirtualBox icons for your Vyatta routers, select your Vyatta router icons, and choose **Device | Change Symbol**. You can then select a regular router symbol to represent your Vyatta routers.

Link interface **e0** of **Vyatta1** to **e0 Vyatta2**, then link interface **e1** of **Vyatta1** to interface **f0/0** of your Cisco router and interface **e1** of **Vyatta2** to interface **f0/1** of your Cisco router.

I would suggest that instead of starting all routers at once, you select router **Vyatta1** then select **Device | Start**. Wait until you see the **Vyatta login:** prompt, then start the remaining routers.

Once all routers are running, you can now configure IP addresses on your routers. Here is a sample configuration that will work so that the routers can ping each other:

- **Cisco Router R1**

  R1#configure terminal

  R1 (config) #*interface f0/0*

  R1 (config-if) #*description Connects to Vyatta1 e1*

  R1 (config-if) #*ip address 10.1.1.1 255.255.255.0*

  R1 (config-if) #*no shutdown*

`R1(config-if)`*#exit*

`R1(config)`*#interface f0/1*

`R1(config-if)`*#description Connects to Vyatta2 e1*

`R1(config-if)`*#ip address 10.2.2.1 255.255.255.0*

`R1(config-if)`*#no shutdown*

`R1(config-if)`*#end*

R1#show ip interface brief

Interface Protocol	IP-Address	OK? Method Status	
FastEthernet0/0	10.1.1.1	YES manual up	up
FastEthernet0/1	10.2.2.1	YES manual up	up

R1#write memory

- **Vyatta1**

  `vyatta login:` *vyatta*

  `Password:` *vyatta123*

  `vyatta@vyatta:~$` *configure*

  `[edit]`

  `vyatta@vyatta#` *set interfaces ethernet eth0 address 10.0.0.1/24*

  `[edit]`

  `vyatta@vyatta#` *set interfaces ethernet eth1 address 10.1.1.2/24*

  `[edit]`

  `vyatta@vyatta#` *commit*

  `[edit]`

  `vyatta@vyatta#` *save*

  `Saving configuration to '/config/config.boot'...`

  `Done`

  `[edit]`

  `vyatta@vyatta# exit`

  `exit`

  `vyatta@vyatta:~$` *show interfaces ethernet*

  `Codes: S - State, L - Link, u - Up, D - Down, A - Admin Down`

Interface Description	IP Address	S/L	
-------- --	----------	---	---------
eth0	10.0.0.1/24	u/u	
eth1	10.1.1.2/24	u/u	

- **Vyatta2**

  Repeat the configuration for Vyatta1, except use ip addresses of *10.0.0.2/24* for *eth0* and *10.2.2.2/24* for *eth1*

  vyatta@vyatta:~$ *show interfaces ethernet*

  ```
  Codes: S - State, L - Link, u - Up, D - Down, A - Admin Down
  Interface        IP Address                    S/L
  Description
  ---------        ----------                    --- ---------
  --
  eth0             10.0.0.2/24                   u/u
  eth1             10.2.2.2/24                   u/u
  ```

  vyatta@vyatta:~$ *ping 10.0.0.1*

  ```
  PING 10.0.0.1 (10.0.0.1) 56(84) bytes of data.
  64 bytes from 10.0.0.1: icmp_req=1 ttl=64 time=10.0 ms
  64 bytes from 10.0.0.1: icmp_req=2 ttl=64 time=0.000 ms
  ```
  <Ctrl>+c

  ```
  --- 10.0.0.1 ping statistics ---
  2 packets transmitted, 2 received, 0% packet loss, time 1010ms
  rtt min/avg/max/mdev = 0.000/5.000/10.000/5.000 ms
  ```
  vyatta@vyatta:~$ *ping 10.2.2.1*

  ```
  PING 10.2.2.1 (10.2.2.1) 56(84) bytes of data.
  64 bytes from 10.2.2.1: icmp_req=1 ttl=255 time=50.0 ms
  64 bytes from 10.2.2.1: icmp_req=2 ttl=255 time=20.0 ms
  ```
  <Ctrl>+c

  ```
  --- 10.2.2.1 ping statistics ---
  2 packets transmitted, 2 received, 0% packet loss, time 1010ms
  rtt min/avg/max/mdev = 20.000/35.000/50.000/15.000 ms
  ```

Congratulations! You should now have the basic lab for Vyatta Cisco integration. Good luck.

Summary

In this chapter, you have explored some of the more advanced and more difficult aspects of GNS3, but have finished with a very powerful toolkit of devices that you can add to your configurations, including Linux PCs (emulated by either Qemu or VirtualBox), Windows PCs (emulated by VirtualBox), Juniper Junos routers, and Vyatta Routers.

Your GNS3 environment is now ready to tackle some extremely diverse simulations. You may even wish to explore some of the many accompanying online exercises (available `http://www.packtpub.com/sites/default/files/downloads/0809OS_ Chapter`) that can help with your certification goals.

The next chapter deals with matching the hardware of Cisco routers and the many variations of the Cisco IOS with the routers supported by GNS3, and how to find the right IOS with the features you need.

5

The Cisco Connection

Matching the hardware of Cisco routers and the many variations of the Cisco IOS can be daunting. This chapter deals with which routers are supported by GNS3, and how to find the features an IOS you need.

The following topics will be covered in this chapter:

- Cisco routers: emulated hardware
- Cisco IOS

After completing this chapter, you will be able to choose the best router platform and firmware image for your simulated network.

Cisco routers – emulated hardware

Dynamips supports a limited number of Cisco routers: Cisco 1700, 2600, 3600, 3700, and 7200 routers to be precise. These routers were designed with generic off-the-shelf processors with well-known published specifications, so *Christophe Fillot* (the author of Dynamips) was able to write software to emulate these well-known functions well enough to interpret the instruction set from a Cisco IOS image for the precedingly mentioned routers and execute it.

Modern Cisco routers use proprietary ASICs to perform switching, so no one outside of Cisco knows what the functions are. Emulation of these devices is impossible without reverse engineering or otherwise obtaining Cisco's intellectual property.

So that's the way it is for Dynamips. It may not be the end of the story though for GNS3, because GNS3 supports other emulators as well. When Cisco start releasing more routers as Virtual Machines (like Vyatta does) it may be possible that these routers will be able to be integrated into a GNS3 topology. Already the Cisco **Cloud Services Router (CSR)** is available in VM form, but its massive compute and memory requirements (4x CPUs, 4GB RAM) make it a little impractical for the average GNS3 user.

Unless you need to emulate a particular model of router for a particular purpose, such as exploring a particular version of IOS, I suggest your best strategy is to use Cisco 7206 routers, or if you need to use SVI (VLAN) interfaces, use 3725 routers with the NM-16ESW module installed.

The following table shows the router models and interface counts supported by Dynamips:

Model	Fixed ports	WIC	NM	PA (7200)
1710	1FE+1E			
17xx	1FE	2		
2610	1E	3	1	
2611	2xE	3	1	
26x0XM	1FE	3	1	
26x1XM	2xFE	3	1	
2691	2xFE	3	1	
3620			2	
3640			4	
3660	2xFE		6	
37x5	2xFE	3	4	
7206				6

The following table shows the WIC modules supported by Dynamips:

Model	Description (Notes)
WIC-1T	1 serial port
WIT-2T	2 serial ports
WIC-1ENET	1 Ethernet port (1700 routers only)

The following table shows the NM cards supported by Dynamips:

Model	Description (Notes)
NM-1E	1 Ethernet port (2610-2651XM only)
NM-4E	4 Ethernet ports (2610-2651XM only)
NM-1FE-TX	1 FastEthernet Port
NM-16ESW	Switch module: 16 Fast Ethernet Ports
NM-4T	4 Serial ports (36xx, 37xx and 2691 only)

The following table shows the adapter/processor options for the 7200 router supported by Dynamips:

NPEs	I/O Controllers	Port Adapters
NPE-225	C7200-IO-FE (1xFE port)	PA-FE-TX (1xFE port)
NPE-400	C7200-IO-2FE (2xFE ports)	PA-2FE-TX (2xFE ports)
NPE-G2	C7200-IO-GE-1 (1xGE port)	PA-4E (4xEthernet ports)
		A-8E (8 Ethernet ports)
		PA-4T+ (4 serial ports)
		PA-8T (8 serial ports)
		PA-A1 (1 ATM port)
		PA-POS-OC3 (1 Packet-Over-SONET port)
		PA-GE (1 GigabitEthernet port)

Cisco IOS

One feature of GNS3 that you might like to explore is the fact that if your physical topology includes some of the routers and interface options supported by GNS, you can use GNS3 to test various versions of IOS. The trick here is to know which version of IOS is suitable for your needs. The cisco Feature Navigator (available at `http://tools.cisco.com/ITDIT/CFN/jsp/SearchBySoftware.jsp`) can help, but in many cases you can often work out if an IOS image you are using supports the features you need simply by looking at the IOS name. Here is a way to decode image names.

Firstly, you have to understand the groupings of letters in the IOS name. They consist of up to seven major fields followed by a `.bin` extension:

```
[Platform]-[Feature Set]-[Memory location][Compression format].[Train
number]-[Maintenance release].[Train identifier].bin
```

Take the following example:

```
c3725-adventerprisek9-mz.124-15.T10.bin
```

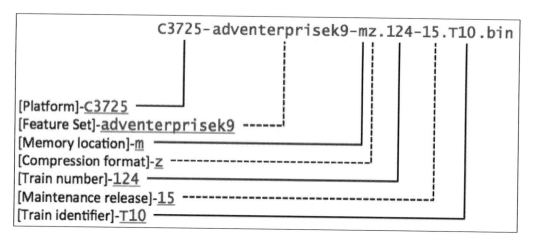

The full name of the image can be seen in the output of the show version command – for the preceding figure it appears as:

```
Cisco IOS Software, 3700 Software (C3725-ADVENTERPRISEK9-M), Version
12.4(15)T10, RELEASE SOFTWARE (fc3)
```

Note that once the image has been decompressed, the information about the compression type and the extension disappear.

Platform

For the GNS3 supported routers, the platform will always be one of the previously mentioned routers – c1700 for the Cisco 1700 platform, including the 1710, 1720, 1721, 1750, 1751, and 1760. A c2600 image will suit all 26xx models, except some images will require more memory to run than is available on the basic 26xx models, hence the XM (extra Memory) in the advanced model names.

Note the Cisco 2691 router requires its own image, it is not really part of the 26xx family and is in fact more like a 3725.

The Cisco 3620, 3640 and 3660 are also considered different platforms, although in GNS3 you can only have one default image for the whole 3600 range.

Similarly, the 3725 and 3745 routers each have their own image, but you can only choose one of them to have a default image for the 37xx range of routers.

The 7206 is the only 7200 series router supported, but the image is consistent for other 7200 models.

Feature set

Since IOS 12.3, the feature set consists of an anchor word followed by options. Prior to 12.3, the anchor word was usually a single letter. The anchor word is usually one of, or a combination of, the words {base, services, advanced, enterprise}. In the preceding example, the anchor word is adventerprise, indicating both advanced and enterprise features.

If the letters k8 or k9 appear in the filename after the feature set identifier, then the image supports encryption, either DES (k8) or 3DES/AES encryption (k9).

Memory location and compression format

The mz sequence always appears as a pair. The m means the image runs from RAM. If you go back far enough, there were some older routers that didn't have enough RAM to run an image, so they ran it from flash memory.

And the z simply means it is compressed in ZIP format.

Train number

Train numbers only change with a major release of code. It is as simple as the version number (without the decimal point) such as the 124 in the preceding example indicating Version 12.4.

Maintenance release

There are usually many maintenance releases of an image in the evolution of a train from one version to the next and the maintenance release appears after the train number in the filename. In the preceding example, 15 is the maintenance release number. In the full name of the image, the maintenance release appears in brackets, such as the (15) in the preceding example.

Train identifier

New releases which contain software fixes and new technology features are referred to as **T-Train** releases and are identified by the letter T (for technology) in the filename and a release number, in the preceding example T10 indicates release 10 of the T-Train. Releases without an identifier are known as **mainline** releases. Mainline do not add new features, they simply fix defects and incorporate features from the parent T-Train.

Sometimes you will find other Trains such as the following:

- **E-Train**: Targets **enterprise** core and SP edge, supports advanced QoS, voice, security, and firewall, and fixes defects.

- **S-Train**: Targets **service** provider markets. Consolidates mainline, E, and other S, which supports high-end backbone routers, and fixes defects.

- **B-Train**: Supports **broadband** features and fixes defects.

RAM requirements and the feature navigator

Different versions of IO require different amounts of RAM to run successfully. Each time you add an image to GNS3, you will notice on the **Edit | IOS images and hypervisors** dialog a link to where you can **Check for minimum RAM requirements** for the image you are dealing with.

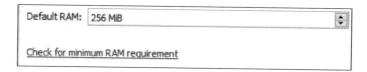

Clicking on this link takes you to **Cisco Feature Navigator**. Here, from the default **Search by Software** tab, you can click on **Search by Image Name**, and enter the image name that you wish to check, such as c3725-adventerprisek9-mz.124-15. T10.bin as used in our examples in this chapter. When you then click on the **Search for Image(s)** button, a list of images that match your search will appear and tell you the minimum DRAM requirements. If there is only a single image match, then full details for that image will appear instead of a list. If you notice that the default RAM you have specified in GNS3 is different to the default RAM shown for your image, you should adjust the settings in GNS3 and save your settings immediately.

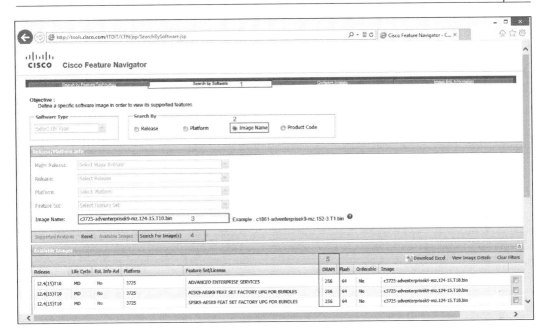

The Cisco Feature Navigator is also useful for exploring which images support which features, and even for downloading the image you wish to test if you have an associated service contract for that image.

Summary

Choosing the best image to use with GNS3 depends on your purpose. If you simply wish to use GNS3 to practice Cisco IOS configuration for certification, then the best strategy is to use Cisco 7206 routers. If you need to use SVI (VLAN) interfaces, use 3725 routers with the NM-16ESW module installed.

If you wish to examine what features are available for a particular router, perhaps because you are prototyping a design, then you can often tell many of the features that are likely to be supported from the name of the image, or use the Cisco Feature Navigator to explore more specific options, including the DRAM required to run a particular image.

In the next chapter, you will get to explore GNS3 internal communications as you examine the many pieces that go together to make GNS3 and how they communicate with each other.

6
Peeking under the GNS3 Hood

If you ever need to debug your simulated topology, it really helps if you know just how the GNS3 orchestra plays together. This chapter deals with the internal communications between GNS3, Dynagen, Dynamips, Qemu, and VirtualBox.

The following topics will be covered in this chapter:

- Understanding the `topology.net` file
- Say hello to the hypervisor
- The GNS3 orchestra
- Debugging using the GNS3 management console

By the end of this chapter, you will have a deeper appreciation of the relationship between the players in the GNS3 orchestra and you will be far better prepared to troubleshoot.

Understanding the topology.net file

By now you will have noticed that when you open a GNS3 project, you have to select a file with a `.net` extension, usually `topology.net`.

Firstly, understand that the topology file does not have to be called `topology.net`. But as GNS3 evolved, it became more practical to simply call the file `topology.net`, and since GNS3 v0.8.3 has only ever saved a **new** topology file as `toplogy.net`. You may find older topologies or even manually handcrafted files, usually with a `.net` extension that will open happily in GNS3.

In fact, the .net file format actually belongs to Dynagen, and you can take any .net file produced by GNS3 and use it directly with Dynagen independently of GNS3. To get a full understanding of the sections of the file that both GNS3 and Dynagen use and interpret, see Greg Anuzelli's tutorial available at: http://dynagen.org/tutorial.htm, but here is a brief overview.

The topology.net file created by GNS3 has two parts. Here is a sample:

```
autostart = False
version = 0.8.4
[127.0.0.1:7200]
    workingdir = C:\Users\chris\AppData\Local\Temp
    udp = 10001
    [[3725]]
        image = C:\Users\chris\GNS3\Images\
          c3725-adventerprisek9_ivs-mz.124-25b.image
        ram = 128
        idlepc = 0x60b1014c
        sparsemem = True
        ghostios = True
    [[ROUTER R1]]
        model = 3725
        console = 2101
        aux = 2501
        cnfg = configs\R1.cfg
        f0/0 = NIO_udp:30000:127.0.0.1:20000
        x = -393.0
        y = -212.0
        z = 1.0
[GNS3-DATA]
    configs = configs
    [[Cloud C1]]
        symbol = Host
        x = -290.5
        y = -219.5
        z = 1.0
        connections = R1:f0/0:nio_udp:30000:127.0.0.1:20000
```

The second part of the file after the [GNS3-DATA] divider (along with the x,y,z values in the first part) are bits of information that the GNS3 GUI needs to recreate the topology drawing, specifically the three dimensional (x,y,z) location co-ordinates of each device. These items are not needed by Dynagen and are purely cosmetic. This part of the file is only created when you save your topology, and can be edited offline – particularly the **x** and **y** co-ordinates if you want to say, have three or four objects evenly spaced across the screen. The **z** parameter is used to place graphical objects (rectangles, ovals, and pictures) in front of or behind each other, and gets changed when you right-click on an object and select **Raise one layer** or **Lower one layer**. Objects that have been lowered to background layers have a negative value for the **z** parameter, but only decoration items (shapes and pictures) can be given a negative z value.

The first part of the file (apart from the x, y, and z values) is the set of instructions that both Dynagen and GNS3 use, and can be seen by issuing the show run command from the GNS3 management **console**.

 If you can't see the GNS3 management **console**, navigate to **View** | **Docks** | **Console**.

The content of this .net file is how the GNS3 GUI stores the information required by the GNS3 console (derived from Dynagen). The lines are largely self-explanatory and it is possible to edit this file if, say, you wanted the console port to be tied to a port other than 2101. In fact, you can create the .net files from scratch if you wish without any help from GNS3, then use standalone copies of Dynagen and Dynamips to run your simulation. This was the standard method of running simulations before GNS3 came along, and is still used by many today.

To explain Dynagen's relationship with GNS3, perhaps a little hypervisor history will help.

Say hello to the hypervisor

When Christophe Fillot began emulating Cisco routers with Dynamips, each instance of a simulated router required its own instance of Dynamips, along with a string of command line options to specify, for example, the amount of RAM, the interfaces, and the virtual connections to other instances of Dynamips. This soon gave way to an improved user interface using a hypervisor approach where a single instance of Dynamips could be initiated which accepted commands over a TCP pipe, usually on port 7200, so chosen because the Cisco 7200 was the first router to be emulated.

For a bit of fun, why not check out the Dynamips hypervisor yourself. From a command line, start Dynamips as a hypervisor running on port 7200 using the command:

dynamips –H 7200

Now start a telnet session to your localhost IP on port 7200:

telnet 127.0.0.1 7200

And finally issue a command Dynamips understands — the command *ethsw create SW1* creates an instance of a generic switch. You should see a reply **100-ETHSW 'SW1' created**. You can try *hypervisor version* as your second command. Successful commands always evoke a reply beginning with **"100"**, including *hypervisor close*.

 You can find out more information by downloading the Dynamips source code, and looking in the README.hypervisor file.

Using the hypervisor approach allowed Dynamips to make many memory efficiencies, and run multiple instances of an image from the same controlling hypervisor. But typing the series of commands required was totally impractical. What was needed was a program that could read a configuration file and pass the appropriate commands to the Dynamips hypervisor.

Enter Dynagen. A program that opens a TCP connection to the Dynamips hypervisor on port 7200, and feeds it a series of commands based on a configuration (.net) file. Dynagen also has a command line console (from which the GNS3 management console evolved) to allow users to type much more human-readable commands for Dynagen to translate into Dynamips speak. Users could now create their own text (.net) files and have Dynagen control the hypervisor. But Dynagen text-file parsing is very unforgiving, and the simplest mistake will reveal:

```
*** Error:  errors during loading of the topology file, please correct
them
```

All that remained was for GNS3 to come along with the GUI interface, which would produce the correct .net file to be passed to Dynagen (far easier than crafting it by hand). This indeed did happen, and over time, Dynagen became incorporated into GNS3 as the **GNS3 management console**.

You can see the interaction between Dynamips and the GNS3 management **console** if you issue the command *debug 3* in the **GNS3 management console** window. You should then see commands and replies being sent to Dynamips, such as (trimmed):

```
sending to dynamips at 127.0.0.1:7200 -> hypervisor version
returned -> ['100-0.2.8-community-x86']
```

The beauty of this approach is that Dynamips doesn't have to be at the IP address of "localhost" or even at port 7200. Potentially you can have multiple instances of Dynamips running at different locations, and listening on different ports, and GNS3 can orchestrate communications between these instances. This concept is explored in more detail in *Chapter 7, Tips for Teachers, Troubleshooters, and Team Leaders*. In fact, you can, and often do, have multiple instances of Dynamips running on your localhost computer because GNS3 will limit the amount of memory allocated to each hypervisor, and spawn a new hypervisor for every different image you use in your configuration. You can see the settings for these values when you choose GNS3 **Preferences** and look at the **Dynamips** settings under the **Hypervisor Manager** tab.

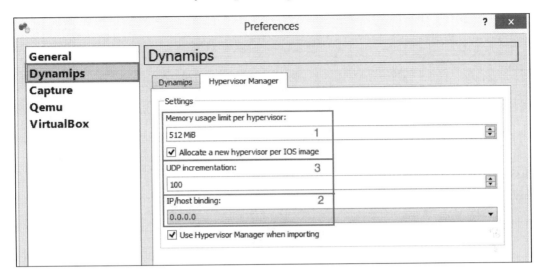

For this exercise, set the **Memory usage limit per hypervisor** to *512 MiB* (1). This means that if you have an image that requires 256MiB per instance, only two images will load before another hypervisor is spawned, and that is a story I will deal with later. For now, just look at simple mathematics and realize that if you are running three identical routers that have been assigned 256MB each, GNS3 will spawn two instances of Dynamips, one listening on TCP port 7200, the other on 7201.

> Normally the amount of memory used by an image is determined by the **Default RAM** allocation specified in **Edit | IOS images and hypervisors**, but can be modified for an individual router in a topology by selecting the router and choosing **Device | Configure**, then select the **Memories and disks** tab, then change **RAM size**.

Also note the other settings in the Dynamips **Hypervisor Manager** setting page: the **UDP incrementation**, and the **IP/host binding**. The **IP/host binding** default value is 127.0.0.1, but I set this to 0.0.0.0 (2) to allow console access to my routers from a remote IP.

The **UDP incrementation** (3) setting is related to another setting on the preceding **Dynamips** tab, the **Base UDP** port. To understand what these settings are for, you'll have to look at exactly what happens when you click and link two routers together. Let me introduce you to the workings of the GNS3 orchestra!

The GNS3 orchestra

The conductor of the orchestra is of course the GNS3 GUI, who wields its Dynagen-like baton — the GNS3 management **console**, to control the three main sections in the orchestra: **Dynamips**, **qemuwrapper**, and **vboxwrapper**. Let me take you through a complex suite with a variety of objects: Cisco routers, generic switches, Qemu devices, and VirtualBox devices. You will observe multiple TCP connections and UDP pipes being created from both the GNS3 management **console** and your operating system's command line. To get a closer look at how the conductor works, open GNS3 to a new blank canvas and issue the command *debug 3* in the GNS3 command **console**:

```
=> debug 3
```

As you open GNS3, the conductor readies the players awaiting your instructions. The moment you drag your first Cisco router onto the workspace, GNS3 spawns an instance of Dynamips and connects to it on port 7200. You can see this in two places:

 To reproduce the effects shown here, use a C7200 router image with 256MB RAM.

1. By issuing a *netstat-a* command in a Windows/Linux/OS X command window:

    ```
    C:\>netstat -an
    ```

    ...

Proto	Local Address	Foreign Address	State
TCP	127.0.0.1:7200	0.0.0.0:0	LISTENING
TCP	127.0.0.1:7200	127.0.0.1:49194	ESTABLISHED
TCP	127.0.0.1:49194	127.0.0.1:7200	ESTABLISHED

2. In the output of the GNS3 management **console**. The following output lines are abbreviated to conserve space:

    ```
    Hypervisor manager: connecting on 127.0.0.1:7200
    Hypervisor manager: connected to hypervisor on 127.0.0.1 port 7200
    ```

    Also in the output of the GNS3 management **console**, note the following (trimmed) lines:

    ```
    Hypervisor manager: hypervisor base UDP is 10001
    ...<snip>...
    PORT TRACKER: allocate port 2101
    sending to dynamips at 127.0.0.1:7200 -> vm set_con_tcp_
    ```

```
port R1 2101

returned -> ['100-OK']

PORT TRACKER: allocate port 2501

sending to dynamips at 127.0.0.1:7200 -> vm set_aux_tcp_
port R1 2501

returned -> ['100-OK']
```

The UDP base port I'll deal with shortly, but notice that GNS3 has told Dynamips to prepare to open ports 2101 and 2501 for console and AUX port communications respectively, which are the base ports defined in GNS3 **Preferences** for the **Dynamips** setting under the **Dynamips** tab. Also note that these ports are not yet opened, in the orchestral analogy you could say they are merely being tuned up at this stage.

Next, add a second router and observe (in the **console** output) that the console and AUX port allocations have incremented by one, but there is no change to the base UDP port.

```
sending to dynamips at 127.0.0.1:7200 -> vm set_con_tcp_port R2 2102

sending to dynamips at 127.0.0.1:7200 -> vm set_aux_tcp_port R2 2502
```

You are about to connect these two devices. Configure them with FastEthernet interfaces if necessary, or use the **FastEthernet Add a link** tool, and connect the two routers. Watch the console output for these lines:

```
Connect link from R1 f1/0 to R2 f1/0

new base UDP port for dynamips at 127.0.0.1:7200 is now: 10002

new base UDP port for dynamips at 127.0.0.1:7200 is now: 10003

sending to dynamips at 127.0.0.1:7200 -> nio create_udp nio_udp0 10001
127.0.0.1 10002

sending to dynamips at 127.0.0.1:7200 -> nio create_udp nio_udp1 10002
127.0.0.1 10001

sending to dynamips at 127.0.0.1:7200 -> vm slot_add_nio_binding
R1 1 0 nio_udp0

sending to dynamips at 127.0.0.1:7200 -> vm slot_add_nio_binding
R2 1 0 nio_udp1
```

And on your host computer, *netstat -an* reveals:

```
C:\>netstat -an | find "1000"
     UDP    0.0.0.0:10001          *:*
     UDP    0.0.0.0:10002          *:*
```

Understanding what is going on here is the key to understanding how Dynamips achieves communication between routers. What has just happened is that a **UDP tunnel** has been created between these two devices.

UDP tunnel concept

Links between devices in GNS3 is achieved using UDP tunnels. What this means in this scenario is that whenever R1 sends a frame from interface f1/0, the entire frame, including the Source MAC address, destination MAC address and payload, gets put inside a UDP packet with a source port of `10001` and a destination IP `address:destination` port of `127.0.0.1:10002` which means that the frame will end up at R2's f1/0 interface because it is bound to port `10002`. The return frames take the reverse path: source port `10002`, destination IP:port `127.0.0.1:10001`.

To illustrate this, I assigned an IP addresses of `1.1.1.1` and `1.1.1.2` to interface **f1/0** on R1 and R2 respectively, then captured a ping packet on the link between R1 and R2 on the host computer's loopback interface. The Wireshark capture shown in the following screenshot shows a ping packet from `1.1.1.1` on its way to `1.1.1.2`, but you can see that the entire layer 2 frame (1), including the layer 2 MAC addresses of R1 and R2 is encapsulated inside a UDP packet travelling from `127.0.0.1:10001` to `127.0.0.1:10002` (2).

```
⊞ Ethernet II, Src: 00:00:00 00:00:00 (00:00:00:00:00:00), Dst: 00:00:00 00:00:00 (00:00:00:00:00:00)
⊞ Internet Protocol Version 4, Src: 127.0.0.1 (127.0.0.1), Dst: 127.0.0.1 (127.0.0.1)
⊞ User Datagram Protocol, Src Port: 10001 (10001), Dst Port: 10002 (10002)
⊞ Ethernet II, Src: ca:00:0c:b6:00:1c (ca:00:0c:b6:00:1c), Dst: ca:01:0c:b6:00:1c (ca:01:0c:b6:00:1c)
⊟ Internet Protocol Version 4, Src: 1.1.1.1 (1.1.1.1), Dst: 1.1.1.2 (1.1.1.2)
     Version: 4
     Header length: 20 bytes
   ⊞ Differentiated Services Field: 0x00 (DSCP 0x00: Default; ECN: 0x00: Not-ECT (Not ECN-Capable Transport))
     Total Length: 100
     Identification: 0x000a (10)
   ⊞ Flags: 0x00
     Fragment offset: 0
     Time to live: 255
     Protocol: ICMP (1)
   ⊞ Header checksum: 0xb78a [correct]
     Source: 1.1.1.1 (1.1.1.1)
     Destination: 1.1.1.2 (1.1.1.2)
     [Source GeoIP: Unknown]
     [Destination GeoIP: Unknown]
⊞ Internet Control Message Protocol
```

Another thing to note is that the first UDP port used was the **Base UDP** port defined in GNS3 **Preferences, Dynamips** settings under the **Dynamips** tab.

Now would also be a good time to issue a *show run* command in the GNS3 management **console** window, to see how GNS3 is building up your topology.net file.

```
=> show run
autostart = False
[127.0.0.1:7200]
    workingdir = C:\Users\chris\AppData\Local\Temp\GNS3_rwftb\working
    udp = 10001
    [[7200]]
        image = C:\Users\chris\GNS3\Images\c7200-p-mz.124-10a.image
        ram = 256
        idlepc = 0x60750000
        sparsemem = True
        ghostios = True
    [[ROUTER R1]]
        console = 2101
        aux = 2501
        slot1 = PA-2FE-TX
        f1/0 = R2 f1/0
    [[ROUTER R2]]
        console = 2102
        aux = 2502
        slot1 = PA-2FE-TX
        f1/0 = R1 f1/0
```

Note that the amount of RAM set for each of these routers is 256MiB. Also recall that in the **Hypervisor Manager** settings previously shown, the **Memory limit per hypervisor** was set to 512MiB.

Now add another router, and watch the **console** output, and check your host computer's TCP connections again with the *netstat -an* command. You will see of course:

```
Hypervisor manager: connecting on 127.0.0.1:7201
```

and…

```
TCP    127.0.0.1:7201       0.0.0.0:0            LISTENING
```

This shows that a second hypervisor instance has been created, and allocated TCP port `7201` for communication. You will also see this reflected in the configuration information if you issue another a *show run* command in the GNS3 management **console** window.

```
...<Output omitted>...
[127.0.0.1:7201]
    workingdir = C:\Users\chris\AppData\Local\Temp\GNS3_rwftb\working
    udp = 10101
```

This also reveals that the base UDP port for this hypervisor is `10101`, recall that the value for the **UDP incrementation** in the Dynamips **Hypervisor Manager** setting page was `100`, so the base UDP port for this instance of the hypervisor is `100` greater than the general base UDP port of `10001` for Dynamips.

You can probably predict what UDP port numbers will be used then if you now connect R2 to R3 with a FastEthernet link. Make the link and see if your prediction was correct:

```
sending to dynamips at 127.0.0.1:7200 -> nio create_udp nio_udp2 10003
127.0.0.1 10101

sending to dynamips at 127.0.0.1:7201 -> nio create_udp nio_udp3 10101
127.0.0.1 10003

sending to dynamips at 127.0.0.1:7200 -> vm slot_add_nio_binding
R2 1 1 nio_udp2

sending to dynamips at 127.0.0.1:7201 -> vm slot_add_nio_binding
R3 1 0 nio_udp3
```

Did you predict that the next connection would be made from port 10003 to 10101? Well done.

But what if you add a switch or a hub? Add a generic Ethernet switch to the topology, and issue a *show run* command in the GNS3 management **console** window. You will notice that there is NO reference to the switch in the output, and in fact if you saved your topology at this point and loaded it later, there would be no switch in your topology. That is because the switch doesn't get allocated to a hypervisor until it has at least one connection to another item in the topology. The question is, since our topology has two hypervisors running, which hypervisor will be allocated the switch?

Connect your recently added switch to R1. Observe what happens in the GNS3 management **console**, and issue another *show run* command in the GNS3 management **console** window. Here is what you are looking for:

Firstly, you should see the connections being created. Note that the UDP port numbers are from the range allocated to the first hypervisor that was spawned, NOT the most recent hypervisor spawned.

```
sending to dynamips at 127.0.0.1:7200 -> nio create_udp nio_udp4 10004
127.0.0.1 10005

sending to dynamips at 127.0.0.1:7200 -> nio create_udp nio_udp5 10005
127.0.0.1 10004
```

Secondly, in the topology description, you can see that SW1 has been assigned to the hypervisor running on TCP port 7200 which allocated UDP ports from the 10000+ range. What actually happens is that GNS3 assigns generic devices like switches, hubs, and clouds to the hypervisor to which the device is first connected.

```
=> show run
autostart = False
[127.0.0.1:7200]
    workingdir = C:\Users\chris\AppData\Local\Temp
    udp = 10001
    [[7200]]
...
    [[ETHSW SW1]]
        1 = access 1 R1 f1/1
    [[ROUTER R1]]
...
```

And finally, if you changed your **Memory usage per hypervisor** setting back on page 73, don't forget to change it back. I recommend setting it to *1024MiB*.

By now you are probably wondering how GNS3 and Dynamips deal with the other supported emulators: *Qemu* and *Oracle VirtualBox*.

Conducting Qemu and VirtualBox

Recall that Dynamips is a hypervisor used to initiate the spawning of Cisco router VMs (virtual machines) instances, and configure host communication to these VMs via console AUX and virtual network interfaces.

Just like Dynamips, both Qemu and Oracle VirtualBox follow a similar hypervisor model, only in this case the hypervisor is "wrapped" to give it similar functionality to Dynamips. The wrappers for the hypervisors are called `qemuwrapper` and `vboxwrapper` respectively, and these wrappers listen on ports `10525` and `11525` as shown in the configuration options in GNS3 **Preferences** under the **Qemu** and **VirtualBox** settings.

Trivia: Port `10525` was chosen by Thomas Pani when he wrote pemuwrapper, the wrapper for the PIX **525** emulator, port `1525` was already assigned by the IANA. Pemuwrapper evolved into qemuwrapper, and when Alexey Eromenko, alias "Technologov" wrote vboxwrapper he simply added `1000` to the qemuwrapper port number.

Again, just like Dynamips, you can run `qemuwrapper` and `vboxwrapper` as standalone applications, then telnet to port `127.0.0.1:10525` or `127.0.0.1:11525` to issue commands like *qemu version* or *vbox version* or the commands to spawn a virtual machine if you bothered to learn the syntax.

Again, like Dynamips, `qemuwrapper` and `vboxwrapper` direct the TCP port to be used for console connections and UDP port for UDP tunnel connections, the base values for these can also be found in GNS3 **Preferences** under the **Qemu** and **VirtualBox** settings.

But unlike Dynamips, the wrapper is NOT the hypervisor as well. The hypervisor is Qemu or VirtualBox, so these applications had to be compiled to allow communication via UDP tunnel interfaces. In the case of Qemu prior to Version 1.1, this required a specially compiled version. The GNS3 downloads page has links to the patched Version 0.11 that I used throughout this book. VirtualBox has built-in support for UDP tunnels.

To see the full GNS3 orchestra playing, you can now add Qemu and VirtualBox devices to your topology and watch the GNS3 management **console** and check your TCP/UDP connections with the *netstat -an* command. As you watch the GNS3 management **console** you will see the hidden power of GNS3 beyond the GNS3 GUI as it conducts its orchestral sections of Dynamips, qemuwrapper, and vboxwrapper to play in harmony, and even see that they have their own sections in the GNS3 `topology.net` file, as can be seen by issuing a *show run* command in the GNS3 management **console**.

So let us take a little closer look at this GNS3 management **console**.

Debugging using the GNS3 management console

You have already seen how useful the GNS3 management console is in observing the inner workings of GNS3, but so far I have only shown you two commands: `debug 3` and `show run`. Using the *help* or *?* command reveals that there are several more console commands:

```
=> help
Documented commands (type help <topic>):

========================================

aux        console  export  idlepc  push      save   stop      ver
capture    copy     filter  import  qmonitor  send   suspend
clear      debug    help    list    reload    show   telnet
confreg    end      hist    no      resume    start  vboxexec
```

Many of these commands are remnants left from the original Dynagen code and have better replacements in the GUI, but sometimes I find it easier to issue a command like `show start` than to check the `topology.net` file in a text editor.

Probably, the most useful commands as far as fine-tuning a router goes are the `idlepc idlemax` and `idlepc idlesleep` commands. Although you can specify values for these items in **Edit | IOS images and hypervisors** settings, if you want to actually experiment with these values, it is far easier to do so here in the GNS3 management **console**.

The final command that I will explore here is the `debug` command itself. If you have been following my directions on your own you will have noticed that the debug messages all begin with a timestamp, then then word `DEBUG(1)` or `DEBUG(2)` (I have trimmed the `Timestamp:DEBUG(x)` sections from my listings to improve readability). Issuing the *debug* command without any parameters explains the meaning of these commands:

```
=> debug
debug [level]
Activate/Desactivate debugs
Level 0: no debugs
Level 1: dynamips lib debugs only
Level 2: GNS3 debugs only
Level 3: GNS3 debugs and dynamips lib debugs
Current debug level is 3
```

As you can see, the console output prefixed with DEBUG(1) are related to Dynamips, while DEBUG(2) are GNS3 related messages.

Summary

In this chapter I have taken a deeper look into the inner workings of GNS3, and in particular its relationship with Dynamips, qemuwrapper, and vboxwrapper. By now you should be familiar with the sections of the topology.net file, how the Dynamips hypervisor functions, the way GNS3 orchestrates communication between devices by managing the TCP and UDP ports used for serial (console) communication and UDP tunnels, the role of Dynamips, qemuwrapper, and vboxwrapper, how UDP tunnels are used to communicate between VMs, and debugging using the GNS3 management console.

In the next chapter, I will show you how to use this knowledge to build multi-hypervisor network simulations spanning several hosts.

7
Tips for Teachers, Troubleshooters, and Team Leaders

Do you need to build a lab with multiple copies of GNS3 working together? Do you want that extra power to expand your horizons, perhaps to use GNS3 control multiple remote hypervisors? These, along with some detailed troubleshooting tips make up this chapter.

Topics covered:

- Packaging your Projects
    - Adding Help
    - Saving Snapshots
- Using remote hypervisors
    - Using VPCS with remote hypervisors
- Running GNS3 in a virtual machine
- GNS3 Limitations
    - Ethernet interfaces always up
    - Cisco router support
    - Host PC communication in a virtual machine environment

- Getting more help

  - ° Official websites for all the GNS3 suite of programs
  - ° Other helpful online resources

After working through this chapter, you will be able to better document your topologies and exercises using the **Instructions** and **Snapshots** features, and you will have mastered multi-machine GNS3 communication and be better prepared to meet those challenging GNS3 lab/classroom environments.

Packaging your projects

GNS3 has a couple of seldom-used features that can be very hard for anyone who wants to set up an exercise to challenge others, or even just to document their own projects. These features are the **Tools | Instructions** feature and the **File | Manage Snapshots** feature.

Adding instructions

A somewhat hidden feature introduced in GNS3 v0.8.4 is the ability to add a page of instructions or documentation to your creations. All you have to do is create a document and save it as `instructions.html` in a directory called `instructions` off your `Project_Name` directory. Next time you open your project, there will be an additional item on the **Tools** menu: **Instructions**.

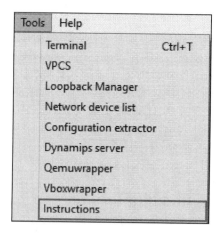

Instructions are ideal if you want to create an exercise, but setting up the initial configuration files for an exercise so that they can't be inadvertently overwritten is more of a challenge. That's where the **Snapshots** feature comes in.

Managing snapshots

The **File | Manage Snapshots** feature is a fancy **Save project as...** option. Choosing **Create** makes a copy of the current **saved** state of your project and puts it in a directory under your `Project_Name` directory. This is ideal for creating a partial topology that can serve as an initial stage of an exercise. Later you can direct students (via the **Instructions** feature) to **Restore** a snapshot to commence the exercise, and possibly even create another snapshot of their completed work for marking.

Using remote hypervisors

In *Chapter 6, Peeking under the GNS3 Hood*, you explored the way GNS3 controls multiple instances of Dynamips and orchestrates communication between them. You can use this knowledge to create rather sophisticated topologies with multiple hypervisors running on multiple computers, all controlled by a single GNS3 central controller.

There are two key concepts:

- Firstly, you will need to know how to run Dynamips as a standalone application on a server. You will also need to store firmware images locally on that server, and know where those images are stored in relation to the server's file system.
- Secondly, you will need to configure GNS3 to be aware of both the location (IP) of the server, and the images stored on that server.

Remote hypervisor tutorial

To complete this exercise you will clearly need at least two computers. A virtual machine or two VMs will suffice, but my example will be based on two remote Dynamips servers, one being a Linux server, the other computer running on Windows. A third computer will be referred to as the **GNS3 host** and is a Windows 8 computer.

Begin by preparing your remote server computers. I will assume that these remote servers already have Dynamips or GNS3 installed. You will not only need to know the IP addresses (or DNS resolvable names), but also the location of a few remote directories. These paths need to be expressed in terms of the remote operating system, using names like C:\Users\user\GNS3\Images or ~/GNS3/Images as appropriate.

Specifically, you will need to know the path to the remote dynamips executable program, the path to a suitable remote Working directory, and the location (and names) of the remote images. In this example these are:

Item	Windows server	Linux server
IP	192.168.0.77	192.168.0.88
Images	C:\Users\user\GNS3\Images	~/GNS3/Images
dynamips	C:\Program Files\GNS3\dynamips-start.cmd	/usr/bin/dynamips
Working	C:\Users\user\AppData\Local\Temp	/tmp

Preparing the remote servers

On the Windows and Linux/OS X servers, make sure your firewall is disabled, or you allow TCP ports 7200-7210, UDP ports 10000-12000, and any TCP ports you wish to be able to use for console access, typically 2100-2120 and 2500-2520 if you use the AUX ports as well.

You can start the Windows server either via GNS3's **Tools | Dynamips server** option, or from a command line. You do not need GNS3 running on this server, so I prefer the command line option:

C:\>"*Program Files\GNS3\dynamips-start.cmd*"

```
Cisco Router Simulation Platform (version 0.2.8-RC6-x86/Windows stable)
Copyright (c) 2005-2011 Christophe Fillot.
Build date: May  1 2013 17:13:19
Local UUID: 85be8a81-5a70-41f8-bcfa-819124d90930
Hypervisor TCP control server started (port 7200).
```

Note that the Windows GNS3 installation supplies a `.cmd` file to launch Dynamips so you don't have to worry about any esoteric parameters.

The Linux server I used did not even have GNS3 installed, but I stored the `Image` files in `~/GNS/Images` for consistency. On Linux/OS X, you need to start Dynamips with the `-H 7200` option:

```
user@linuxmint ~ $ /usr/bin/dynamips –H 7200
Cisco Router Simulation Platform (version 0.2.8-x86/Linux stable)
Copyright (c) 2005-2011 Christophe Fillot.
Build date: July 4 2013 06:16:28
Local UUID: 616638cf-2180-439b-b7d0-f6323436257c
Hypervisor TCP control server started (port 7200).
```

Preparing the host computer

You are now ready to configure your GNS3 host computer with two new external hypervisors and some extra images. It is not a bad idea to test that your host GNS3 computer can connect to the remote hypervisors:

```
C:\>telnet 192.168.0.77 7200
<Enter>
200-At least a module and a command must be specified
hypervisor close
100-OK
Connection to host lost.
```

You are now ready to start preparing the GNS3 host computer. Start by navigating to **Edit | IOS images and hypervisors | External hypervisors** tab. Enter the IP address for one of the external hypervisors, check that the **Port** value is set to `7200` and that the **Working Directory** describes a directory that the remote server understands, such as `C:\Users\user\AppData\Local\Temp` for Windows or `/tmp` for Linux/OS X. Click on **Save** after adding the first external hypervisor before you add the second one.

You have to be careful if you add two external hypervisors sequentially, because the default port numbers shown on the form increment automatically. To reset the port numbers to their original values, click on the Hypervisor you just added in the list on the right-hand side, then edit the values as shown in the following screenshot:

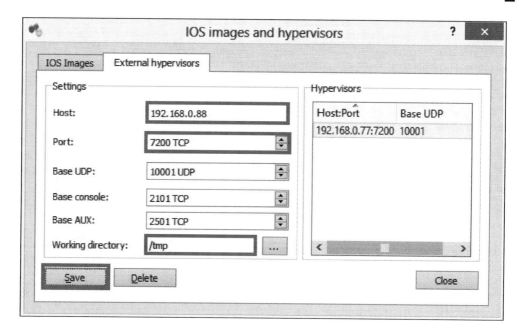

Once you have saved both external hypervisors, you will now need to specify which images exist on these remote servers, so while remaining in the **IOS images and hypervisors** dialogue, select the **IOS Images** tab.

 If you are planning to run more than one image type on the remote server, I recommend you add at least one remote hypervisor (running on different ports) for each image you wish to run remotely on that server.

Firstly, check to see if you have a local **Default image for this platform** for an image you are about add.

If you do, you must select it from your list of **IOS Images** (1) and clear the **Default image for this platform** field (2) and click on **Save** (3), otherwise you will never be able to add your remote images to your topology. This also conveniently fills the fields for **Image file** (4), **Base config** (5), and **IDLE PC** (6), which you can now edit if necessary. Note that the **Image file** name (4) must reflect the file structure of the remote hypervisor, while the **Base config** (5) is a file local to the GNS3 host. However, **before** you click on **Save**, you must ensure that the **Use the hypervisor manager** field (7) is cleared, then select the remote hypervisor (8) you wish to configure from the list of hypervisors, then finally click on **Save** again (9).

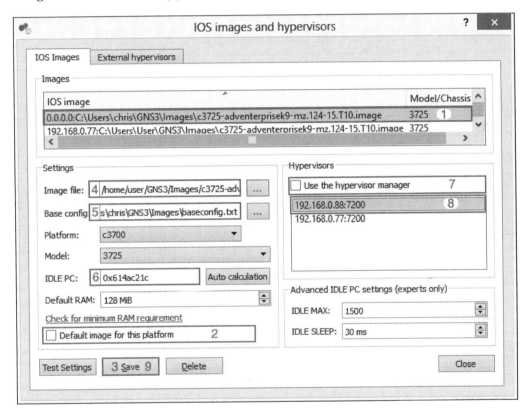

If you don't have a local copy of the image you are adding, then you can ignore steps 1-3 as shown in the preceding screenshot, but you will manually have to fill in the fields for **Image file** (4), **Base config** (5), and **IDLE PC** (6) — you can't use the **Auto calculation** for a remote image.

Load balancing across multiple hypervisors

In the previous example, note that two hypervisors are shown in the list of hypervisors (8). It is possible (perhaps too easy) to select multiple hypervisors and assign them to an image, and GNS3 will load balance new router additions across the hypervisors. However, if you do choose to load balance across multiple hypervisors, you **must be careful** to ensure that all the hypervisors use the same local path to the image file.

Using your local GNS3 host as a hypervisor

If you wish to use images on your host GNS3 computer as part of your topology, you must also set up a hypervisor bound to your Ethernet IP address, and use that. Otherwise, when you connect your locally hosted router to a remotely hosted router, GNS3 will send the remote hypervisor a command (following command) which the remote hypervisor will interpret as "connect myself to myself".

```
nio create_udp nio_udp1 10001 127.0.0.1 10001
```

Furthermore, you will also need to run Dynamips as an independent process **before** you add a router using your local IP's hypervisor. GNS3 can only automatically start hypervisors that belong to `127.0.0.1`. Conveniently, in the Windows version of GNS3 there is a shortcut to start an independent hypervisor; you can reach it via **Tools | Dynamips server**. Non-Windows users will have to resort to a *dynamips –H 7200* command.

Building the topology

I recommend issuing the *debug 3* command in the GNS3 management **console** before adding routers to your topology.

Assuming you cleared the **Default image for this platform** option for the image you are about to add, the first thing you will notice when you add the image is that you are presented with a dialog asking you to choose which image you wish to add.

When selecting remote images, keep in mind that any traffic between instances is going to travel over UDP tunnels. This means that any TCP traffic travelling between two remote images will be tunneled in UDP. It also means that if you have a topology with remote images residing on different remote servers, or even a mixture of local and remote images, they will be subject to the maximum MTU of the path between these sites. This may mean that any large frames may get fragmented, unless you can adjust the MTU on your Dynamips servers and between sites.

In other words, I recommend that you keep your whole topology on a single remote server if possible, or if you plan to use multiple remote servers, have the remote servers as close as possible to each other.

Choosing the right platform

In theory, hypervisors can be run on Windows, Linux, or OS X and be managed by a single copy of GNS3 running on any platform. However, you may find that connections suddenly drop out or disappear, or devices will not connect for any apparent reason.

In my experience, I have had most success running remote hypervisors and local hosts on Linux platforms, and most difficulties with Windows platforms.

Using VPCS with remote hypervisors

When you are using remote hypervisors in your topology, it is possible to still use VPCS (the Virtual PC Simulator, discussed in *Chapter 3, Enhancing GNS3*) but your configuration is a little different.

Firstly, you will need to decide on which server you are going to run VPCS. For this example, I will assume that the VPCS application will be running on the same computer as the GNS3 application, and that computer has an IP address of 192.168.0.22, and we intend to connect VPC1 to a router running on a remote server at 192.168.0.77.

In GNS3, when you are preparing the NIO_UDP settings for the VPCS cloud connection, you can't use `127.0.0.1` as the remote host. From a remote hypervisor's point of view, it needs to know the IP address where VPCS is running, so in this example you would use `192.168.0.22` as the **Remote host**.

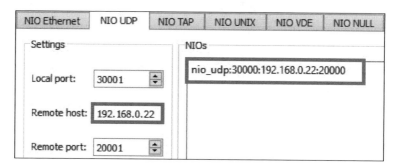

For the second half of the connection, you will have to manage the remote ports for each VPCS virtual PC. For the connection shown previously that will send packets from a source port of `30000`, you would configure VPC1 with the IP of the remote server hosting this connection, in this example, `192.168.0.77`.

VPCS [1] > *set rhost 192.168.0.77*

VPCS [1] > *show ip*

NAME   : VPCS [1]

. . .

LPORT   : 20000

RHOST:PORT   : 192.168.0.77:30000

If controlling multiple remote instances of Dynamips from a single controlling copy of GNS3 is not what you want to do, but you still want to connect multiple topologies together, then running GNS3 in a virtual machine may help.

Running GNS3 in a virtual machine

Many GNS3 users like the idea of keeping the simulation environment on a separate virtual machine. This partly arose because early versions of GNS3 and even Dynamips were less stable on Windows platforms, or perhaps it was more a case of having a more detrimental effect on the underlying platform when the program crashed. Whatever the reason, running GNS3 in a virtual machine, typically Linux based, is a popular way of running GNS3.

The GNS3 WorkBench solution

GNS3 WorkBench is one such example of a packaged virtual machine running GNS3 on a Linux base. GNS3 WorkBench is a free download available from my blog site at `http://rednectar.net/gns3-workbench` and comes with prepackaged tutorials. In this section I will describe how I have connected multiple copies of GNS3 working together by using GNS3 WorkBench installed on Windows computers.

Scenario: You have multiple Windows computers on which you wish to run GNS3, perhaps a lab or a classroom setup. You have two major requirements:

1. The host computers must be able to communicate (ping, telnet, and so on) with the routers in the topology. It is a well-known shortcoming of the GNS3 environment that Windows host computers have unreliable connectivity to devices even if they are connected via a direct Ethernet connection.

2. The GNS3 environment needs to be hosted in such a way that every GNS3 host can communicate with every other host so that UDP tunnel connections can be made between GNS3 instances.

To achieve the first requirement, you could either configure MS Loopback interfaces on your Windows hosts (as described in *Chapter 3, Enhancing GNS3*), or run GNS3 in a Virtual Machine on the Windows host. In this example, I used a Linux VM running under VMware Player achieve the result. The following diagram shows how the Windows computer has its Ethernet adapter configured with an IP address of `172.16.11.10`, and is using the GNS3 router as its default gateway of `172.16.11.1`. The Linux host does not need an IP address on its **eth0** interface. The VMware Network Adapter has been bridged to the Windows Ethernet adapter, which needs to be connected to an external switch to ensure that the adapter is active.

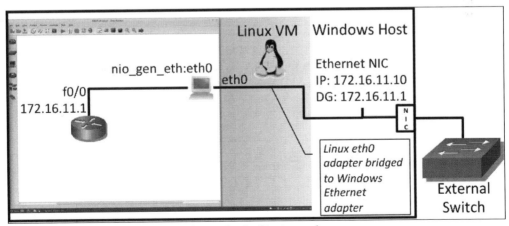

Source: lewing@isc.tamu.edu

Achieving the second requirement is a little trickier. I achieved this by creating a VLAN Ethernet adapter: **eth0.255** on the Linux VM and assigned an IP address of `192.168.255.xx` to this adapter. This allowed all the hosted VMs connected to the **External Switch** to communicate with each other over VLAN 255, while keeping the Windows host computers isolated from each other. The following figure shows how two Windows computers on different subnets and therefore different VLANs can be connected to the external switch using 802.1Q VLAN trunk ports, allowing the hosted VMs to still communicate via VLAN 255. Each copy of GNS3 has a serial connection to the other via a NIO_UDP connection that makes use of this VLAN 255 connection.

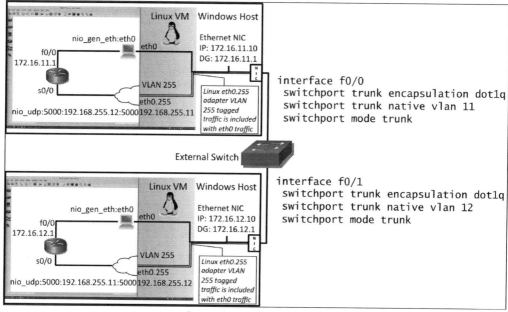

Source: lewing@isc.tamu.edu

The switch port has (in Cisco language) the **native VLAN** configured. This is how you can control which other ports on the network can see this traffic. Configuring the native VLAN of any two (or more) ports to be on the same native VLAN allows you to allow those devices to share a subnet, effectively turning your switched network into an electronic patch-panel.

At the same time, the Linux virtual machines need to have a common communication channel (a common subnet/VLAN) to enable any two routers to create a NIO-UDP tunnel (via a cloud connection) between them, such as a serial connection. By giving each Linux host a VLAN interface, in this example on VLAN 255 and an IP addresses on VLAN 255, every Linux host can communicate with every other, and therefore NIO_UDP interfaces can be created between any two devices. Such interfaces are useful for serial connections, but could also be used for Ethernet connections if desired.

GNS3 Limitations

This preceding design was created in part to overcome the inability for a host computer to be able to communicate with a guest router. However there are some other limitations that you should be aware of as well.

Ethernet interfaces are always up

On a normal physical network, the state of a point-to-point Ethernet interface is dependent on the state of the other end. If one end is shut down or unplugged, the other end is also in a **down** state. This has implications for routing fail-over scenarios as well as other protocol-timeouts.

In GNS3/Dynamips, if one end of a point-to-point Ethernet link is shut down, it has no effect on the other end. Your topology will be dependent on protocol timeouts or you will need to configure SLAs to trigger fail-over scenarios.

In fact, even if no cable is attached to an Ethernet interface, it will remain in an **up** state from the moment the `no shutdown` command is issued.

This means that if you want to test fail-over scenarios on GNS3 in the same way you would in a lab, by shutting down an interface or by removing the cable, you are out of luck. This method won't work in GNS3.

If you want to simulate a true point-to-point routing simulation, then use serial interfaces to make these connections. In the case of serial interfaces, if one is shut down, then other end goes down too.

Cisco router support

The fact that Dynamips only supports specific routers is often seen as a crippling limitation for GNS3. Recall that the reasons for this were discussed in *Chapter 5, The Cisco Connection*. However, remember that by using Cisco 7200 series routers in your simulations you can still practice your configurations using IOS versions up to 15.x.

Host PC communication in a virtual machine environment

As explained in *Chapter 3, Enhancing GNS3*, creating a cloud connection from a router directly to a host's Ethernet interface does not guarantee communication between the router and the host, even if the IP addressing is correct. Also explained in that chapter, creating loopback interfaces and bridging them is one way of solving this problem. Running GNS3 within a virtual machine as explained previously is another way of getting around this problem.

Getting more help

I am sure you will come across other problems that you will need to solve that I haven't been able to cover in this book. Here are a few places where you can look for help by including, for example site: `forum.gns3.net`, as part of your search criteria when you go looking for help.

Official websites for all the GNS3 suite of programs

The official websites for GNS3, Dynamips, Dynagen, VirtualBox, Qemu, and VPCS are shown in the following table. However, for GNS3 related information, the best starting place is the GNS3 forum, and the best way to search the forum is sadly *not* using the search function on the forum website, but by including the words **site:forum.gns3.net**, as part of your search criteria in a Google search.

If you cannot find an answer, then by all means post a question on the forum, but you might want to read `http://forum.gns3.net/topic3178.html` before posting to ensure you get a more positive response.

Site title	Location
GNS3 official site	`www.gns3.net`
GNS3 Forum	`forum.gns3.net`
Dynamips	`www.ipflow.utc.fr/index.php/Cisco_7200_Simulator` and
	`7200emu.hacki.at/`
Dynagen	`dynagen.org/`
VirtualBox	`www.virtualbox.org/`
Qemu	`wiki.qemu.org/`
VPCS	`http://wiki.freecode.com.cn/doku.php?id=wiki:vpcs`

Other helpful online resources

The prime site for GNS3 news is the GNS3 forum: `http://forum.gns3.net/`. Click on the **View active topics** link and keep up-to-date with discussions about future changes and see the problems that others are experiencing. You may even be able to help others!

Often overlooked are also the official documentation and video sites: `http://www.gns3.net/documentation/` and `http://www.gns3.net/video-tutorials/` respectively. Or you can go directly to the youtube site: `http://www.youtube.com/user/GNS3Talk/videos`

One of the best sites for free labs is René Molenaar's `http://gns3vault.com/`. You have to register to get to the free labs.

There are several Facebook pages that claim to be associated with GNS3. These can dribble some interesting tidbits to you News Feed along with some advertising posts as well. The official page is `https://www.facebook.com/gns3official`, and you can follow the official twitter feed at `https://twitter.com/gns3_official`.

If you are using GNS3 for Cisco certification, don't forget Cisco's learning network, you will find many posts about GNS3 at `http://learningnetwork.cisco.com/`.

Many blog sites have articles occasionally on GNS3 related topics. Often these sites are the blog sites of regular GNS3 forum contributors, such as `http://brezular.wordpress.com/`, `http://www.gns3-labs.com/`, `http://www.nowindows.net/wp/`, `http://commonerrors.blogspot.com.au/` and of course my own `http://rednectar.net`.

Summary

This chapter completes the journey of exploration through GNS3 from installation through running multiple hypervisors to finally multisite and interconnected GNS3 configurations. If you have grasped the difficult concepts in this chapter you should now be able to manage a topology using remote hypervisors, including using VPCS in the mix, build a lab of interconnected computers running GNS3 in a virtual machine, be aware of how to best work around some of GNS3's limitations, and know how to search for more help.

You will probably find yourself coming back to this book to explore a little more about installing on a different operating system, using a different emulator, getting tips on building your ultimate lab or even just to check on the variations of Cisco routers that are supported. If you are studying for certification, I hope you will find the online exercises useful and even getting to understand how GNS3 works will help you with your studies

Don't forget to explore the *Preparing for certification using GNS3* online chapter (available at `http://www.packtpub.com/sites/default/files/` `downloads/0809OS_Chapter 8_Preparing_for_Certification_using_GNS3.pdf`) and complete some of the many accompanying online exercises found there, especially if you are preparing for CCNA, CCNP, or CCIE certification.

Index

Symbols

100 percent CPU utilization problem
avoiding 39-41

A

access port type 59
ASA firewalls, with Qemu
ASA binary, unpacking 74
IP addresses, configuring 76, 77
Qemu/ASA Preferences, configuring 75
topology, creating with ASA 76
ATM switch 45
Auto calculation feature 17
AUX port 63

B

base config feature 18
BES 76
bridge-utils package 52
B-Train 102

C

Cisco ASAs 68
cisco Feature Navigator
about 99
URL 99
Cisco IOS
about 99, 100
compression format 101
feature navigator 102, 103
feature set 101

maintenance release 101
memory location 101
platform 100
RAM requirements 102
train identifier 101
train number 101
Cisco routers 97, 98
cloud device 48
Cloud Services Router (CSR) 97
commit command 84
configs directory 29
cpulimit 76

D

device console
accessing, remotely 65
troubleshooting 63
dot1q port type 59
Dynagen
about 106
URL 133
Dynamips
about 8, 97, 110, 115
adapter/processor options, for 7200 router 99
NM cards 98
router models 98
URL 133
WIC modules 98
Dynamips hypervisor
overview 107-109

E

Ethernet switch 42-44
EtherSwitch router 60
E-Train 102

F

FastEthernet 111
frame-relay switch 45

G

Generic Ethernet switch 59
generic switches, GNS3
  about 42
  ATM 45
  Ethernet switch 42-44
  frame-relay 45
Gnome Terminal 8
GNS3
  about 7, 67
  accessing 64
  applications 8, 9
  downloading 11
  enhancing 47
  generic switches 42
  installing 13
  installing, on Linux Mint 13
  installing, on OS X (Macintosh) 12, 13
  installing, on Windows 11
  Instructions page, adding 120
  limitations 131
  Manage Snapshots feature 121
  official websites, for programs 132
  online resources 133
  post installation tasks 14
  pre-installation tasks 8
  prerequisites 9
  running, in virtaul machine 128
  supported emulators 8
  URL 8
  URL, for downloading 11
  URL, for forums 133
  URL, for official site 133
GNS3, limitations
  Cisco router support 132
  ethernet interfaces always up 131

host PC communication in virtual machine
    environment 132
GNS3 management console
  used, for debugging 117
GNS3 orchestra
  about 110, 111
  Qemu, conducting 116
  UDP tunnel concept 112-114
  VirtualBox, conducting 116
GNS3 router
  connecting, to LAN 48-50
GNS3 topologies
  linking, on different hosts 66
GNS3 WorkBench
  about 129
  solution 129, 130
Graphical Network Simulator. *See* GNS3
graphics
  adding 64
GUI
  about 30
  objects, aligning 31
  text, adding 30

H

hypervisor
  local GNS3 host, using as 126

I

idlepc idlemax command 117
idlepc idlesleep command 117
Idle Program Counter (Idle-PC) 41
installation, GNS3
  on OS X (Macintosh) 12, 13
  on Windows 11
installation, GNS3 on Linux Mint
  Dynamips, installing 14
  GNS3, installing 14
  repository, preparing 13
  VPCS, installing 14
  Xterm, installing 14
installation, GNS3 on OS X (Macintosh)
  GNS3, installing 13
  Wireshark, installing 12
  XQuartz X11, installing 12
Instructions page

adding, in GNS3 120
iTerm2 8

J

Juniper routers 68
Juniper routers, with Qemu
  IP addresses, configuring 83, 84
  Junos, installing 79-81
  Junos source image, patching 79
  Qemu/JunOS Preferences, configuring 81
  required files, preparing 78
  topology, creating with Junos router 82
Junos 10

K

Konsole 8

L

LAN
  GNS3 router, connecting to 48-50
Linux Mint
  GNS3, installing on 13
Linux NIO TAP adapter
  about 52
  bridge, configuring 53
  bridge, creating 53
  bridge-utils package, installing 53
  cloud device, connecting 54
  connectivity, testing 54
  IP address, reassigning to br0 53
  NIO TAP device, configuring 54
  tap interface, configuring 53
  tap interface, creating 53
  uml-utilties package, installing 53
Linux PC, on Oracle VirtualBox 89
load balancing
  across multiple hypervisors 126
local GNS3 host
  using, as hypervisor 126

M

mainline releases 101
Manage Snapshots feature, GNS3 121
Microcore Linux

used, for obtaining Qemu 70
Microcore Linux, with Qemu
  configuration, saving in Microcore Linux
      72
  IP addresses, configuring 72
  Qemu guest, downloading 70
  Qemu preferences, configuring 70
  topology, creating with Qemu box 71
Microsoft Loopback adapter 52

N

Netgroup Packet Filter. *See* NPF interface
Network Interface Card (NIC) 48
NM-16ESW card 60
NPF interface 50

O

Olive 78
OS X
  GNS3, installing on 12, 13
OS X TUN/TAP adapter
  about 55
  bridge, configuring 56
  bridge, creating 56
  connectivity, testing 57
  IP address, assigning to bridge0 57
  tap interface, configuring 56
  tap interface, creating 56
  TunTap package, installing 55

P

packets
  capturing, with Wireshark 37-39
pcap 51
Pemu 8, 67
physical interfaces
  connecting to 48
PIX 525 emulator 116
port types
  access 59
  dot1q 59
  qinq 59
post installation tasks, GNS3
  Setup Wizard 15
prerequisites, GNS3

CPU 9
memory 9
router image files 9, 10
Private Package Archive (PPA) 13
project
conceptualizing 28
opening 29
packaging 120
project conceptualization
about 28
configs directory 29
topology.net file 28
working directory 29
PuTTY 8, 11

Q

Qemu
about 8, 67, 116
obtaining, Microcore Linux used 70
URL 133
Qemu 0.11.0
downloading 68
installing 68
Qemu emulator
about 68
ASA firewalls, adding 73
Juniper routers, adding 78
Qemu support, adding 68
Qemu preferences 69
Qemu support 68
qemuwrapper 68, 110, 116
Qinq 59

R

remote hypervisors
using 121
VPCS, using with 127, 128
remote hypervisor tutorial
about 121
host computer, preparing 123-125
load balancing, across multiple hypervisors
126
local GNS3 host, using as hypervisor 126

platform, selecting 127
remote servers, preparing 122
topology, building 126, 127
router configuration
about 22, 25, 26
routers, adding to topology 23, 24
routers, connecting 24
routers, starting 25
saving 27
workspace, opening 22, 23
router image file 9, 10
routers
VPCS, connecting to 33
routers management
tips 32

S

SecureCRT 8
Setup Wizard
about 15
base config, checking 18, 19
Idle-PC value, configuring 17
image file, selecting 16
settings, saving 17
S-Train 102
SuperPutty 8, 11
SuperPutty troubleshooting 26

T

TeraTerm 8
terminals
features 61
terminal tips
about 61
AUX port, using 63
device console, troubleshooting 63
different terminal application, using 62
text
adding 64
Topology Graphic View window 27
topology.net file
about 28, 105
parts 106, 107
T-Train releases 101

U

UDP tunnel 112-114
uml-utilties package 52

V

vboxwrapper 110, 116
VirtualBox
  about 8, 67, 116
  URL 133
  used, for adding Vyatta router 89-94
VirtualBox emulator
  about 84
  VirtualBox Support, adding 84
virtual machine
  GNS3, running in 128
Virtual PC Simulator. *See* VPCS
VLAN support
  adding 59
VPCS
  about 9
  connecting, to routers 33
  host devices, adding to topology 33
  installing 14
  renaming 33
  routers, configuring 35, 36
  URL 133
  using 32
  using, with remote hypervisors 127, 128
VPCS application
  starting 34, 35
Vyatta 10
Vyatta router
  adding, VirtualBox used 89-94

W

Windows
  GNS3, installing on 11
Windows PC, on Oracle VirtualBox
  about 85
  GNS3, configuring 87
  topology, creating with VirtualBox host 87,
    88
  Windows XP virtual machine, creating 85,
    86
Windows Telnet client 8
WinPcap 11, 50, 51
Wireshark
  about 9, 37
  installing 12
  used, for capturing packets 37-39
working directory 29
workspace management
  tips 31, 32

X

xdotool 84
XQuartz 12
XQuartz X11
  installing 12
Xterm
  about 8
  installing 14

Thank you for buying
GNS3 Network Simulation Guide

About Packt Publishing

Packt, pronounced 'packed', published its first book "*Mastering phpMyAdmin for Effective MySQL Management*" in April 2004 and subsequently continued to specialize in publishing highly focused books on specific technologies and solutions.

Our books and publications share the experiences of your fellow IT professionals in adapting and customizing today's systems, applications, and frameworks. Our solution based books give you the knowledge and power to customize the software and technologies you're using to get the job done. Packt books are more specific and less general than the IT books you have seen in the past. Our unique business model allows us to bring you more focused information, giving you more of what you need to know, and less of what you don't.

Packt is a modern, yet unique publishing company, which focuses on producing quality, cutting-edge books for communities of developers, administrators, and newbies alike. For more information, please visit our website: www.packtpub.com.

About Packt Open Source

In 2010, Packt launched two new brands, Packt Open Source and Packt Enterprise, in order to continue its focus on specialization. This book is part of the Packt Open Source brand, home to books published on software built around Open Source licences, and offering information to anybody from advanced developers to budding web designers. The Open Source brand also runs Packt's Open Source Royalty Scheme, by which Packt gives a royalty to each Open Source project about whose software a book is sold.

Writing for Packt

We welcome all inquiries from people who are interested in authoring. Book proposals should be sent to author@packtpub.com. If your book idea is still at an early stage and you would like to discuss it first before writing a formal book proposal, contact us; one of our commissioning editors will get in touch with you.

We're not just looking for published authors; if you have strong technical skills but no writing experience, our experienced editors can help you develop a writing career, or simply get some additional reward for your expertise.

open source
community experience distilled

Learning OMNeT++

ISBN: 978-1-84969-714-9   Paperback: 460 pages

Make realistic and insightful network simulations with OMNeT++

1. Create a virtual Network Simulation Environment rapidly

2. Focus less on the theory and more on results, with clear, step-by-step instructions, previews, and examples to help you along the way

3. Learn how to run and analyze a Network Simulation

Mastering Nginx

ISBN: 978-1-84951-744-7   Paperback: 322 pages

An in-depth guide to configuring NGINX for any situation, including numerous examples and reference tables describing each directive

1. An in-depth configuration guide to help you understand how to best configure NGINX for any situation

2. Includes useful code samples to help you integrate NGINX into your application architecture

3. Full of example configuration snippets, best-practice descriptions, and reference tables for each directive

Please check **www.PacktPub.com** for information on our titles

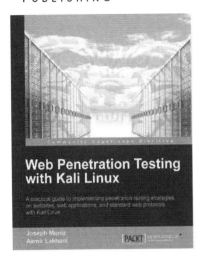

Web Penetration Testing with Kali Linux

ISBN: 978-1-78216-316-9   Paperback: 342 pages

A practical guide to implementing penetration testing strategies on websites, web applications, and standard web protocols with Kali Linux

1. Learn key reconnaissance concepts needed as a penetration tester

2. Attack and exploit key features, authentication, and sessions on web applications

3. Learn how to protect systems, write reports, and sell web penetration testing services

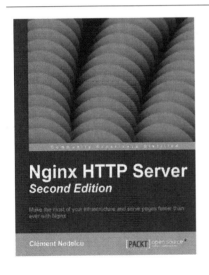

Nginx HTTP Server - Second Edition

ISBN: 978-1-78216-232-2   Paperback: 318 pages

Make the most of your infrastructure and serve pages faster than ever with Nginx

1. Complete configuration directive and module reference

2. Discover possible interactions between Nginx and Apache to get the best of both worlds

3. Learn to configure your servers and virtual hosts efficiently

4. A step-by-step guide to switching from Apache to Nginx

Please check **www.PacktPub.com** for information on our titles

Made in the USA
San Bernardino, CA
22 July 2015